TO SWEETEN ALABAMA

A Story of a Young Man Defying the Odds

Anthony Daniels Jr.

authorHOUSE®

AuthorHouse™
1663 Liberty Drive, Suite 200
Bloomington, IN 47403
www.authorhouse.com
Phone: 1-800-839-8640

First published by AuthorHouse 5/20/2009

ISBN: 978-1-4389-4457-9 (sc)
ISBN: 978-1-4389-4458-6 (hc)

Printed in the United States of America
Bloomington, Indiana

This book is printed on acid-free paper.

ALLEGIANCE

This book is dedicated to my grandparents, the late Willie Mae and Willie James Dubose Sr., for instilling hard work, respect, and honesty within me during my childhood, which has made me the person that I am today. I love you and miss you immensely.

I also dedicate this book to my parents, Gertrude and Anthony Lee Daniels Sr., for their love and support. I want you two to know that I love you with all of my heart.

CONTENTS

FOREWORD

The human spirit never ceases to amaze me.

Our history books are filled with stories about people who despite their circumstances managed to overcome incredible odds. Each of them liberated themselves from the worst enemies of mankind: ignorance, poverty, disease, illiteracy, self-doubt, addiction and hopelessness. All of us are beholden to their examples as we do our very best to find purpose and meaning in our own lives.

As an educator and advocate for public education for over thirty years, I have embraced one simple creed: there is no hurdle high enough that adversity can create that education and hard work cannot overcome.

I will never forget, many years ago, as a high school student, I took a test at the Department of Employment Security in my home state of

Illinois. I was looking for a job, and I went there in hopes of securing one. The person who interpreted the results of the test concluded that the only jobs for which I would ever qualify would be those that required the use of my hands.

This opinion, quite frankly devastated me. But I didn't let it stop me. I knew that my life could never be defined by one test or someone's opinion of my potential. So I worked even harder than before, and exceeded expectations. I graduated from high school and went on to college and graduate school.

Today, I am the former president of the largest teacher's union in the country. I am here today because I learned that success has never been handed to anyone on a silver plate. Men and women who refused to give up have clawed out of adversity.

This is why I am so excited about this book. Although Anthony grew up poor and with an uncertain future, he held on to the principle that our beliefs about ourselves are what a rudder is to a ship: they control the direction and destiny of our lives. Anthony's story cuts deep into the heart and mind of a young man who decided that he would not be defined by circumstance, or by what others had expected of him. He chose to be defined by grit and an unwavering focus on his dreams.

From the first day that he began his tenure as Chairman of the NEA Student Program, he was determined to be the best at his job and lay a solid foundation for those that would hold his position after him. Under his watch he helped our organization raise the level of awareness on the college affordability issue. Our student membership not only experienced an unprecedented increase during his tenure but we also saw an overwhelming number of students becoming active and engaged members. He developed and nurtured relationships with key Congressmen on Capitol Hill that allowed him the access to advocate on behalf of students across the nation.

But more important than all of his successes as a young professional, he is a man of great wisdom, character and integrity. I know for sure that he will continue to dedicate his life to the millions of students around the nation who are living with the unconfirmed hope that they will also have the opportunity to live their dreams.

This book offers a great example for how all of us can transcend the walls of adversity in life and see what is waiting for us on the other side. Anthony's impressive journey of success over poverty, fear of rejection, and self-doubt uniquely qualifies him to share his story with the world.

A story is told about two frogs that fall into a jar of milk. One says, "What a misfortune! I'll never get out of here alive!", and after a few futile attempts, gives up and drowns. The other one struggles and paddles all night long, adamant that he will get out. As the day dawns, his determination has churned the milk into butter, and he is able to crawl to freedom - the stumbling block has become the stepping-stone.

Be determined to rise.

INTRODUCTION

It has only been one generation since my family moved from the Sehoy plantation in Guerryton, Alabama. They spent years toiling under conditions of humiliation and oppression. They shared countless stories with me about the horrible living conditions of the plantation. For them, school was secondary. The plantation was their life.

I can remember one story in particular where the rain would make it so difficult for them to travel the dirt road that they would have to make hand bridges in order to cross over to the other side. But despite these conditions, my grandmother and grandfather stood strong and never allowed those things to break their spirits or define who they were as human beings. I have never forgotten those stories. And I have used them to energize and inspire me to live with honor, discipline, and focus in all that I do.

In addition to my family's personal trials and experiences, I have also been moved by a timeless story once told to me. The story is told of a father teaching his son about the fundamentals of farming. The father tells the son, "To get the best production out of the land you must plow in a straight line." The son then asked, "How do you plow in a straight line." The father replied, "The only way you can plow in a straight line is to pick a point out on the horizon, fix your eyes on it and don't ever stray from it."

This has been the philosophy of my life since I was a young boy. I have always picked goals on the horizon that were bigger than what the world or anyone else thought I could achieve. I have never strayed from what I knew was possible for my life. And I have never believed in defeat or retreat. My mind and heart only knows victory and to not surrender.

We all have a path in this life. We just have to decide whether we are going to see our own path through the eyes of grasshoppers or giants. I decided long ago that I was a giant and that I would never live a mediocre life. In everything we do, we must endure and persevere no matter how hard it gets or how long it takes. Charles Haddon Spurgeon said, "By perseverance the snail reached the ark." We need to be like that snail.

I decided to write this book in early 2007, about a year into my term as Chairperson of the National Education Association Student Program. It was during this time that I reflected on losing my grandmother, coping with failure, living in six different households from fifth grade to twelfth grade, to not having any direction, to graduating from college, and then becoming the first African American male ever elected as Chairperson of the National Education Association Student Program. All of these things have shaped who I am and I have never been ashamed to tell anyone about my past. We are all the sum total of our experiences and choices we make in this life.

I attribute much of my tenacity to my grandparents who taught me about the authority of faith and its ability to activate the power of God. It is everything that I am and everything that I will be. When others gave up on me, it was my faith that carried me. When I wanted to give up on myself, it was my faith that lifted me up. God never quits on us. Whatever he has begun in us, he will see it through until we have reached and fulfilled our purpose. I am reminded every day of what God says in Proverbs 3:6, "In all thy ways acknowledge him and he shall direct thy paths." I hope my story will inspire you to live big and to think bigger than what you can see in front of you. Because as the saying goes, sorrow looks back, worry looks around, and faith looks up.

MEMORIES OF MY LIFE AND FAMILY

I was born in Bartow, Florida, a small city southwest of Orlando. This small city had the closest hospital specializing in obstetrics, just 20 miles away from Haines City, Florida, where my parents lived. After just two months in Haines City, Florida, my parents decided to take me to live with my maternal grandparents in Midway, Alabama. They were confident that my grandparents could take better care of me until they became financially stable. Prior to my birth, my parents had already been struggling financially with two other children.

My grandparents' home was located in a community on a hill called Shady Mountain; their house had four bedrooms with about ten other people living there. Shady Mountain was relatively small, with seven other households just like my grandparents'. As I grew and became acclimated to my new environment, I started to refer to it as "The Hill," which became my home. Shady Mountain evolved as a community from previous sharecroppers who had lived and worked on a plantation called "Sehoy." The people of this community were like family and I can still remember names and characteristics today. For example, Mrs. Martha Rogers was a very nice woman that lived down the street. I was a friend of her grandson. Another person in the community was Mrs. Jackson, who kindly transported my grandmother to the grocery store on a monthly basis. She was also a very nice woman.

Directly at the bottom of the hill, this small community housed only two convenience stores and two stop signs. There weren't any traffic lights or paved roads. At night, the area looked like one giant farm. My grandma was heavily relied upon within the community because she spent much of her time ensuring that everyone in the family had all the bare necessities such as food, clothing, shelter, toiletries, comfort, love, and happiness. Grandma planted fruit and vegetables in the garden every summer: greens, black-eyed peas, onions, tomatoes, bell peppers, and watermelon. In addition to the vegetable garden, there were three fruit trees: pear, plum, and peach. To add to our "farm" life, we had two family pigs in the backyard and a pet chicken we named Muffen. He always pecked at anyone wearing stonewashed jeans or jackets. We always found Muffen's mannerisms to be humorous.

Grandma made the majority of the decisions in the household, because Granddad was disabled at the time. He broke his pelvic bone after he fell riding a horse in his earlier days, confining him to a wheelchair. Eventually his condition worsened; due to the poor circulation in his legs, his left foot had to be amputated.

Although times were often hard in Alabama, Grandma was such a strong, influential figure in society because everyone respected her opinion and took her advice. People viewed her as a wise and humble woman. She was able to instill in me a strong work ethic along with strong faith and morals. Her lessons taught me about perseverance and commitment.

My grandparents became very attached to me and treated me as if I was their own child, especially my grandmother who often called me her favorite. As I got older my parents made several attempts to take me back to Florida, but each time my grandparents contested the idea. They had created a stable family environment with nurture and love; moving away would have disoriented me at the vital age of learning and growing, both mentally and emotionally. Before I came to Alabama, my sister Stephanie, who is only eleven months older than me, also lived with my grandparents on Shady Mountain for the same reason, but she returned to Florida with my parents shortly after she started walking. After her departure, my grandmother was devastated. She vowed that they would never house another grandchild only later to have them taken away. This was the main reason why I stayed in Alabama and didn't return home to my parents.

My parents' strong interest in actively getting me back caused me to feel tense and uneasy. Once or twice a year they would come to visit me, but because they had been absent from my life for so long,

I treated them as if they were strangers. When I was a child, I would go to the back of the house and hide when strangers came to visit. I often thought they were like my biological parents, coming to take me away.

Throughout my childhood, I always considered my grandparents to be my mother and father and I was determined not to let my birth parents change that.

It was a struggle trying to identify who my birth parents were and who my caretakers were, but living poor in Midway was definitely another prominent struggle that affected my life. Many would think it's nearly impossible to survive without a car, but Grandma dispelled that rumor. She refused to allow not having a car to become an excuse for taking care of the family. Granny was a hard worker and made things happen. There were many people in the community that shared my grandmother's ideals of kinship, which enabled the community to have such a strong working unit within. She believed in treating everyone fairly and helping those in need. She helped to create special bonds and relationships within our community that many thought were unbreakable. Because the community was made up of so many genuine, caring people, it made life without a vehicle more manageable. Our neighbors would drive my grandma wherever she needed to go in order to get items for the household, pay a bill, attend an occasional doctor's appointment, and even be present for church.

Looking back on our financial struggles helps me to appreciate where I have come from, and also to appreciate the human spirit of kindness and generosity. Without experiencing these struggles, I may have never learned the skills of true teamwork and kinship to help my fellow neighbor. As I mentioned before, the entire community acted as a working unit to ensure that every member within Shady Mountain was provided with resources and necessities to survive comfortably. It was without a doubt that whenever our family or household needed something from the community, someone was always willing to lend a helping hand to make sure we got it and vice versa.

My grandma was the strongest woman in the community. More importantly, she was the strongest person that I have ever met in my life. Her godliness, wisdom, and knowledge were infectious and everyone was blessed in her presence. I believe that she was an angel picked right out of heaven's front door. She had an undying love for people and everyone respected her. With all of the misfortune, inequality, and hatred in the world, it seemed as though nothing ever really bothered her because her faith in God was so strong, which was all she needed to face each day. One example of her relentless faith occurred whenever she yawned. After every yawn she would say, "Lord, thank you Heavenly Father, don't leave me." Just a simple bodily function reminded her that the Lord was always with her, which enabled me to believe that the Lord is always with me, too, and all of us.

My grandmother, Mrs. Willie Mae Dubose, was the most remarkable woman in the world. Her remarkable contributions included providing food, shelter, wisdom, guidance, and strength not only to her family but also to the entire community. Through her strong faith in God, Granny would see things others wouldn't and couldn't. She would discipline me when I needed it, but she did not withhold her nurturing love. Often times she went to the local convenient store and bought my favorite candies on credit. The only individuals that could buy something on credit were those few who were trusted and well respected in the community. These well-respected members of society were generally the older members with several generations of descendents. My grandmother, being one of these trusted members within the community, had the privilege to use her discretion as to who could use her credit in this particular convenient store. All purchases that were made on credit to that person's name would first have to be cleared by the individual whose name was on the books. The clerk would call the credit holder to confirm that the purchase was true or the clerk would accept a note from the credit holder. Both means of communication between the clerk and credit holder would also serve as a confirmation. Therefore, I was often able to make purchases in the store without the presence of my grandmother. I felt very proud that my grandmother was just as loved, trusted, respected, and appreciated within the community as she was within my heart.

Prior to attending grade school, an additional member of the family came into the household. My Aunt Barbara, Grandma's youngest child among eight, was attending Alabama State University in Montgomery, Alabama. She attended the university for a short period of time, where she was working toward a bachelor's degree in Early Childhood Education. Unfortunately, Aunt Barbara's journey ended prematurely after she witnessed a murder on the doorsteps of her dormitory. Even though my grandmother was a strong woman who generally overcame adversity, she was protective of her children and now concerned about Aunt Barbara's safety. After Grandma was notified of the murder on Aunt Barbara's campus, she immediately requested that Aunt Barbara get her bags and be ready to come home. Grandma found Aunt Barbara a ride home.

At times during my childhood there were some days I looked forward to, especially during the summer. Fridays were always rewarding. On this day, there was a very nice, older white couple, Mr. and Mrs. Locklar, who drove a mobile grocery store that we called "The Rolling Store." At this time many families did not have transportation to travel into town to buy the necessary items their families needed. Therefore, the rolling store provided these families with the opportunity to purchase groceries and other household items. Most days I would be outside playing sports or building something when it was time for the rolling store to arrive. My friends and I would have a friendly bet to see who could spot the rolling store first. Once we saw the rolling store at the bottom of the hill we would immediately stop playing and begin running to our houses to inform our grandparents. While running to our separate homes you could see the dust sweltering in the air, while the sound of our bare feet echoed from the hard dirt roads. This sent a sound of childhood excitement throughout the neighborhood.

The rolling store also extended a line of credit to my grandparents until the end of the month. They sold goods such as candy, chips, bread, bologna, sausage, dish and laundry detergent, baking flour and meal, honey buns, grapes, bananas, apples, oranges, orange-aide juices, and the list goes on. My favorite things to buy as a kid was orange-aide, honey buns, skittles, and candy cigarettes. All the kids in the neighborhood anticipated the arrival of the rolling store each Friday. It was the highlight and the perfect treat to end each week.

Along with being able to purchase my favorite treats at the rolling store, lighting fireworks was another favorite pastime of mine. My friends and I saved our money to purchase fireworks and candy cigarettes. We had competitions with skyrockets on whose would travel the highest or stay in the sky the longest. At the same time we would smoke our candy cigarettes. A lot of the adults were smoking real cigarettes around us. We knew it was bad, but we felt rebellious emulating their behavior.

Even the children in our community were familiar with one another. All of us would meet up around 8 a.m. every morning to play under a huge pine tree closest to Grandma's house. Grandma could watch me play from where she sat on the front porch. My friends and I would build houses and cars and pretend that we were actors on television. We would pretend to be driving those cars or living in those houses, and even acting out scenes from church service and television. I enjoyed the days when I was driven by my imagination and make-believe.

Throughout the day, we would go back to our homes to get snacks for lunch and afterward resume playing. We spent a lot of time building basketball hoops out of milk crates. We would rip out the bottoms of the crates so that there was an opening on both sides. We would then engage in a full court game; each of us pretending to be high school basketball stars or NBA stars. I can remember calling myself Cottontail. Cottontail was the local high school basketball star. Or whenever we had company around, I would call myself Magic after Ervin "Magic" Johnson who started for the Los Angeles Lakers. Several members of my family played high school and college basketball and because of their influence, basketball was my main sport of interest growing up.

When we weren't playing basketball, we played football and baseball in a 100-yard plowed field. A typical day in Midway was like a day in the dessert: hot, humid, and dry. Imagine playing football or baseball for three to four hours when the sun is at its peak. Because of the heat and constant activity, I was a scrawny kid with a fast metabolism. We also went hiking and bird hunting with BB guns, often competing to see who could kill the most birds. We played outdoors from sun up to sun down and even then our families would have to force us to come into the house in order to get ready for bed. Every morning at 8 a.m. was the beginning of a new adventure. "The Hill" was all we knew, but not having anywhere else to go allowed us to expand our imaginations and enjoy the purity of childhood.

CHILDHOOD

I entered kindergarten in the fall of 1987. It was a new and exciting endeavor for me. My first teacher was Mrs. Raybon at Merritt Elementary in Midway, Alabama. Midway's population was under 5,000 at the time. Many people I have met in life have had the opportunity to attend a Head Start program, where young children can receive early exposure to academics and the social arena of public schooling. I, on the other hand, didn't have that same opportunity. Therefore, my exposure to school was a bit frightening at first due to my lack of preparation in both social and learning skills.

I went into this new environment with a classroom of twenty total strangers. One thing I did learn very quickly was discipline. Corporal punishment was in full effect in Mrs. Raybon's class. I often received punishment in the form of a fat pencil square on my knuckles. I received this form of punishment many times after excessive talking. After receiving several knuckle bashings, I started to stay focused on my tasks.

I vaguely remember my first and second grade years, but my third grade year I remember distinctly. I had another great teacher who reminded me of how a little boy should behave himself in school. My third grade teacher was Mrs. Ramsey. She had high standards for all of her students and expected us to do our very best at all times. It was this class that gave me a strong foundation for work ethics in school. I can remember starting the year off in a group that performed at a lower level than everyone else. This group was called the "Blue Birds." As the year progressed, I started to perform at a higher level. I eventually made it into the group that was known as the smart group, the "Red Birds." It was in the third grade where, with the help and persistence of Mrs. Ramsey, I learned how to push myself and identify my academic strengths and weaknesses. She encouraged me to do my best. With her guided practice, I could see my independent skills flourish.

However, fifth grade posed a serious challenge for me. I became intrigued and slightly influenced by the negative attitudes of a group of boys that had been retained. This new group of kids I was starting to hang out with consisted of ten guys who were habitual repeaters. Some of those boys had been retained in the fifth grade at least twice. Even though I had worked so hard to progress academically, I continued to hang out with them. Unfortunately, the more we hung out the more I started to lose my drive in school, which was reflected in my grades. My attitude toward school had become relatively similar to the attitudes of my new peers. I can remember times when the teachers would tell me that I wasn't doing anything in their classes besides sleeping. The school informed my Aunt Barbara that I had become a great sleeper and daydreamer. It had become evident that I was going to fail fifth grade along with my new friends. In addition to all of my troubles with school, little did I know that this would be the year I would endure one of the worst experiences of my life.

One afternoon, I came home from school and was surprised to see my grandmother's son – Uncle Bob, who lived about two and a half hours away from us in Birmingham, Alabama – sitting in the living room. Soon the rest of my uncles and aunts, who lived throughout the state of Alabama, came to visit as well. I began to question the cause for this random gathering. "What is going on and why is everyone down here?" My Aunt Bobbie asked me to go into the back room and continue to wait. She said she would talk to me later. After waiting anxiously, she came back to see me. I immediately thought something was wrong. My Aunt Bobbie said, "Roger, your grandmother has been diagnosed with liver cancer and the doctor has only given her nine months to live." The nickname Roger came from my Uncle Larry, who had started calling me this during my primary years. After receiving the bad news I cried and called on God, asking him to spare my grandmother. I was frustrated and concerned about my grandmother; therefore my behavior and attitude began to change. I became very reserved and stopped hanging out with my new crew of friends. I also became more alert and focused in school. No one could begin to imagine how difficult it was for me – a young boy losing the person that had raised him since he was two months old. This news was a devastating blow to me mentally, emotionally, and spiritually. I didn't think it was fair that my grandmother was leaving us so soon. I couldn't imagine living my life without her.

As a result of my failing grades, I ended up not being promoted to the next grade. I didn't fail the fifth grade because I didn't know how to do the work; I failed the fifth grade because I had come to believe that doing well in school wasn't cool. The remainder of my classmates went onto the next grade and left me behind. This became the most discouraging time in my life.

Due to Grandma's sickness, she had become bedridden and less active. She stopped going into the garden and even outside all together. Much of her time was spent praying in her bedroom and very rarely, occasional walks around the community. On Sundays people that knew my grandmother would come by to have a conversation with her and sometimes give her some money for support. These visits and times of condolences went on throughout the entire summer. In addition to all of the non-family visitors, my uncles and aunts would visit her more frequently throughout the weeks before her passing. Although Grandma's sickness was progressing internally, she never allowed others to see it bother her, at least not during that summer. I decided to take on all of the chores that needed to be done in the house even though my grandmother told me that I didn't have to. At this time Grandma and I started having conversations about her sickness. I would ask her about it and she would respond by saying, "Son, I'm going to be okay, you shouldn't worry about me."

One day, my Uncle Bob came in from Birmingham to visit us. He began to talk to me about life. He reminded me that I could be anything I wanted to be but I had to do one thing. He said, "Roger, you have to take your school work seriously." He then asked me, "What do you want to be when you grow up?" I replied, "A basketball player." He then said, "Tell me how many basketball players you know that didn't go to college first." Uncle Bobby Lee stated, "Son, you have to make good grades in order to make it to college or even be a basketball player." I said, "I want to be an NBA player or a lawyer." He spoke for over an hour and I listened to him intently. Throughout the lecture, I did not make eye contact. Instead, I sat with my head hanging low, my eyes toward the floor. Even though I was being reprimanded, I was more than ready to get started on my journey. The journey he was describing. I can't remember all the details of what was said but I do recall the importance and especially the statement, "Do it for your grandmother; make good grades for your grandmother."

That last statement stuck with me. I decided that I would do my absolute best throughout the upcoming school year. I also decided to part ways with my old friends and hang out with the smart people.

Months passed by and there were just days left before I was to return to the fifth grade for the second time. This was a new beginning for me – a fresh start and a time to show everyone that I could do whatever I set my mind to. Conveniently, all my teachers from the previous year had been transferred to another school. This was all great news to me, but for others it wasn't so great. No one around me liked change. They were afraid of anything that was out of the norm. Their minds were conditioned to think that the faculty, policies, and procedures should remain the same as they were when previous generations attended. The year went on and I made excellent grades. Being the teacher's helper each week and also performing well in my classes rewarded me. My teachers were fairly young, though very charismatic, enthusiastic, and competent. All of the encouragement, feedback, and support I received enabled me to earn the A&B honor roll by the end of the first six weeks.

The same day I received my A&B honor roll report card I enthusiastically got off the bus at the bottom of the hill and ran from the bottom of the hill to the top without stopping until I reached the porch. I opened the door and raced to the back of the house and yelled, "Grandma! Grandma! I made the honor roll!"

Although Grandma was in a lot of pain, she looked at me with a smile and said, "Good job, baby." This made my day, seeing the smile on her face. I was filled with joy, hope, and prosperity.

As the semester went on, things started to work out in my favor academically, but not emotionally. School got out for the semester due to Christmas recess. However, during the Christmas break the amount of traffic in Grandma's house had increased dramatically; family, friends, and associates started to visit my grandmother more often to bring her gifts. Surprisingly, at least for me, Ms. Locklar from the rolling store came by to bring her some oranges.

While it was tradition that most of our family came during the holidays, it was good to see those that usually only came during the Fourth of July, which is when we have our family reunion. This particular Christmas was unusual; usually everyone was happy and filled with joy, but unfortunately this time around there was a lot of crying and praying. This indicated to me that Grandma didn't have much time left. On Christmas Day my Uncle Dubose, who was a deacon for our church, requested that the entire family meet at Grandma's house. The family arrived and my uncle prayed for Grandma and the rest of the family. Then the holiday recess was over and school resumed.

The second semester began and I returned with the same determination I had before the Christmas recess. This semester was supposed to be the semester that the grades played basketball against each other. It was the beginning of February when the fifth and sixth graders began practicing to play against each other. Although the school had yet to decide on a date and time for the game, everyone was still excited. Every day after school I would remind Grandma of my basketball game and she assured me that she would be there to support me. Classes were going well, but things worsened at home. Soon the school notified us of a date for the fifth versus sixth grade basketball game. They decided to have the game on Saturday, March 26th. Once I found out I informed Grandma and the rest of the family. Everyone was excited about coming to see my game.

It was the week of March 20, 1994, when I found Grandma humming an unfamiliar song over and over again. I can even recall the stanza of the song: "Come by here my Lord. Come by here. Come by here my Lord. Come by here. Oh Lord, come by here. Somebody's praying Lord, come by here. Oh Lord, come by here." Routinely, I heard this for a few days; it was odd because she never sang this before.

In Grandma's room there were two beds, one for each of us. The next morning, I got out of bed and looked over at Grandma and said, "Everything is going to be okay. Don't worry." She became very teary-eyed but didn't respond. That evening, I got home from basketball practice and Grandma was still on bed rest, humming the same song from the nights before. It was hard watching the cancer take the best of her. Days went by. The day of my first basketball game was steadily arriving. Although I was feeling even more anxious and excited for the game, I was becoming more and more concerned about my grandma's health. The morning before the game I looked over at Grandma and called to her, "Grandma, everything is going to be okay." This time there was no response, not even a tear in her eye. I called her name twice. I went over to her bed and shook her, but still no response.

I immediately called my aunt in the room and said, "Grandma won't answer me." She said to me, "Roger, Mama is gone, she's gone." Everybody in the house began crying and screaming at the top of their lungs. The ambulance came to pick her up and pronounced her dead at the Bullock County Hospital. I felt like my mother had been taken away. Despite the circumstances, I still played in the basketball game the following day. I went to the game with the attitude of winning and doing my very best. I finished the game with 18 points and led my team to victory. Although Grandma wasn't there, I felt as though she would've wanted me to do my best. Her angelic spirit was certainly with me that day, as it will always be.

After the funeral, my parents asked me if I was ready to come home and I told them, "No." I spent the remainder of my fifth grade year with my Uncle Dubose and his family. Aside from my recent loss and grief, I was proud that I had been promoted to the sixth grade. The next challenge was to prepare for the upcoming summer, when I was to move to Florida to live with my parents.

MY LIFE IN FLORIDA

I went to live with my parents after almost eleven years of living with my grandparents. The move to Florida was a bit of a culture shock among many other things because the fast city life was different from the stagnant and slow progressing Midway, Alabama. As the summer went on, the thought of moving back to Alabama crossed my mind several times; almost every day. My two cousins Jamaal and O'Neal helped to alleviate my struggle through this transition; they were also from Alabama and had traveled to Florida that summer to visit nearby relatives. Unfortunately, that same summer, my cousin got himself into some serious trouble during an Independence Day celebration. He and a couple of his buddies were apprehended and convicted of capital murder. They were later sentenced to thirty-three years in prison at the age of sixteen. My cousin's arrest was unfortunate to bear witness to, but it did not influence my behavior. For the remainder of that summer, my cousin Jamaal and I continued to play as children do. The 1994-1995 school year was fast approaching and my parents hadn't uttered a word about both my living and school arrangements.

That fall, my parents enrolled me at Shelley Boone Middle School in Haines City, which was about a mile from my house. Previously, in Alabama, I had attended an all-black school. That first day at Shelley Boone gave me insight into a completely different culture, one in which I was exposed and expected to interact with children of all races for the first time in my life. Due to the blanket of racism in Alabama, I often felt inferior to the white race; however, through my grandmother's teaching of her faith, I learned to embrace all races equally. Even though this was the first time I'd ever attended an integrated school it didn't take me long to get to know my classmates. For the first time in my life I felt like the minority in school. I began to experience the effects of racial discrimination through verbal statements, like when one of my white peers, Martin, said to me, "Your grandmother was my grandfather's slave." This particular boy did not know my situation or me, but still agonizing over my grandmother's death, I felt compelled to retaliate. Martin's comment felt like salt on an open wound. I later learned that Martin was a product of ignorance; through this understanding and mercy, Martin and I became friends.

One year later, as I began the seventh grade, I became interested in playing recreational sports within the community. First I played football for the 140-pound minimum weight limit team, which was primarily for eighth graders and larger-sized seventh graders. Playing football kept me away from my previous friends, which in turn kept me out of trouble.

The football season usually lasted for about two months, which overlapped into basketball season. Unlike city league football and basketball, all of our regular season games were within the city. The majority of my time was spent playing basketball and the remainder of the time I spent studying. Therefore I had no time to engage in ignorance. The season went on and soon it was time for the All-Stars. As I was a 6-foot, 2-inch point guard averaging around 18 points a game, I became a pretty popular guy in the city. At the end of every season, the coaches would choose an All-Star team that would represent the entire city league for particular age groups. Thankfully, I was the number two pick for the All-Star team, where my position was the shooting guard. On most teams, coaches would select players of my height to play center or forward but I was an exception to this stereotype. In my case, I played in the position in which I played my best, guard. I played guard on offense and center and forward on defense. The first tournament we played in was the Polk County Recreational All-Star Tournament. In order for my team to advance to compete at the state level, we had to win in the county. And we did – we won the bid for the state tournament! After the folks back in Haines City heard the news, they decided to sponsor our team's hotel rooms, meals, and Gatorade.

We left Haines City for Pompano Beach, where the state tournament was to be played. My teammates and I entered this

31

tournament without any reputation because no one had ever seen us play. The first two games of the tournament we blew our opponents out by approximately 20 to 30 points. But with the Osceola Magic, we met our match.

The game was intensely close from the tip-off down to the very last second, as both our teams exchanged basket for basket. Ultimately, we lost the championship game by two points. We left the game extremely sad and disappointed because we had played with our hearts down to the wire. The van ride back to Haines City was quiet and long. No one wanted to talk or even be bothered. Yet although we were heartbroken, we didn't come back empty-handed; we brought back the runner-up trophy and the city celebrated our accomplishment. After the All-Star season was over, I received an invitation to play Youth Basketball of America (YBOA) and Amateur Athletic Union (AAU) Basketball. This would require some traveling, and so I was able to practice basketball every day of the week except for game days. The season lasted until August, when we played in the YBOA national basketball tournament in Polk County at the area high schools. My participation in basketball took up so much of my personal time that the only spare time I had was for going to school.

Just like any other small town or urban area, the cities were generally separated by socioeconomic status. Haines City was no different. I felt sorry for many of my teammates because they were surrounded by more negativity than I was. Many of them lived in the heart of the twin poisons: alcohol and drugs. The basketball gym we would practice in was surrounded by boarding homes. Boarding homes were set up like the floors of a hotel. The floor would have at least four to five individual rooms, which were usually rented out by drug dealers.

It was sad that a friend of mine would actually rent out one of these rooms in a boarding house or use his father's room. Occasionally, following practice I would visit a couple of my friends in their rooms in these boarding houses. I always felt very uncomfortable in these houses due to the overwhelming amount of illegal drugs that they had in their rooms. I never understood why young men in middle school had to resort to selling drugs. I tried initiating conversations with some of them but the most popular reply was, "I got to get that money man." It is hard to admit, but I could definitely see how selling drugs lured some of my teammates and peers, because at such a young age many were loaded with cash. I had even entertained the thought of choosing that path as well, but I always knew it wasn't right. I would often ask myself, "Why would you sell something that would harm another human being?" It was this type of questioning and rationalization that helped me fight any bit of temptation to do something to hurt others and myself.

During the eighth grade, I started to get a lot of attention from high school coaches in both basketball and football. But in the midst of all of this, I was still thinking about moving back to Alabama. I had conversations with my sisters and other relatives about this possibility. My sisters weren't as supportive of the idea of me moving back to Alabama, but other relatives expressed their hopes for me and encouraged me to continue to believe that anything was possible. Like many people, I found comfort and peace in my faith. I relinquished all my hopes, fears, and aspirations to the Lord through prayer. Starting from the sixth grade I prayed about moving back to Alabama. I missed my old life in Alabama. I wanted so badly for my life to resume back to the way it was. For years, I always asked God to deliver me from this place. Even with the acceleration of my talents in basketball, my life wasn't the way I would've wanted it to be. I began to pray even harder throughout my eighth grade year.

As my eighth grade year continued, I became very popular in athletics all throughout the school. I was receiving recognition from the principal, the teachers, and the students. I was often challenged to a basketball game by random people. Some of the students in my school had started skipping their physical education classes in order to watch me play ball against members of the faculty. From the way the students treated me I felt as though I had already made it to the NBA. Unfortunately, though, my discipline on the basketball court did not transfer into the classroom and I had a hard time separating productive class time with socializing.

Mr. Belisle, my eighth grade science teacher, was rather funny but strict. His raspy tone will forever be engrained in my mind. "Welcome to detention, Mr. Daniels," he stated as I walked into the room. "Sooner or later we could just add an hour to the school day for you." I must admit I did talk a lot. Mr. Belisle definitely made sure I received an ample amount of punishment for my disruptive behaviors.

Later during the school year I became close friends with several different cliques. I was becoming interested in a more diverse crowd. I hung out with the "nerds" and "geeks" from my advanced classes. I also hung out with the jocks that I played sports with. Lastly, I called the guys from my neighborhood my homeboys. I defined homeboys as people I hung out with regularly after school hours.

My social life was starting to take precedence in my life. I began to hang out and sleep over friends' houses on the weekends that I didn't have basketball games. I used to go over to my friend Jay's house, where many of my closest friends went. It was quite the experience hanging out at Jay's house. He and his family had things that I could only dream about. They had a swimming pool, jet skis, a pool table, and video games. The good thing about hanging out at Jay's was that we got up on Sunday mornings and went to church. Going to Jay's church was an awesome experience. It helped strengthen my faith and keep me focused on my priorities. My favorite part of Sundays with Jay occurred after church, however, when we played full court basketball.

Being close friends with Jay gave me a fresh and positive perspective of what the definition of family should be. The image of Jay's family is one I will never forget. Jay's dad, Dan, and his mom, Patsy, were excellent examples of a nurturing and loving family environment. Their values and successes reminded me of *The Cosby Show* because they emulated an organized and functional family. I appreciated that they actually ate dinner at the same dinner table together. There were a number of things that stood out to me with this family that have never personally occurred with my own family or households. For example, they ate breakfast, lunch, and dinner together at the table. They also attended church together every Sunday. Jay's mother stayed at home and tended to the house and everyone's needs within it. I admired the love and support they showed each other.

In eighth grade I grew nearly an inch taller than I was in seventh grade: 6 feet, 2 and 3/4 inches tall. This was the same year that NBA star Tracy McGrady played at Mt. Zion Academy in Durham, North Carolina. My eighth grade teacher was also a basketball coach at the time. He tried to get me to play basketball at Auburndale High School, and then possibly transfer to Mt. Zion after my sophomore year. I entertained the idea of pursuing that path, but ultimately my mind was still focused on playing basketball in Alabama.

That summer coaches and basketball pundits continued to inquire about my future plans. Three weeks into the summer, I convinced my parents to allow me to go to Alabama for the rest of the summer. To my advantage, it didn't take long before the head coach of Bullock County High School in Midway; Alabama received word about how well I could play basketball. Later that summer I asked my parents if I could live in Alabama, but they were indifferent. In order to influence their decision, I began to tell them about my unhappiness living in Florida. My Uncle Dubose, whom I lived with directly after my grandmother's death, also knew about my misery in Florida and he helped convince my mom to let me stay. Since my grandmother's death I had lived in Florida for three years but never considered it my home. I felt incomplete and unhappy. Finally, my chance of returning to Alabama had come. I had been praying about this since Grandma died and now my prayers were answered.

HIGH SCHOOL YEARS

My first day of high school was somewhat scary. I was the new kid on the block – again. After about two weeks, the head varsity basketball coach and athletic director, Coach Huffman, requested that I come to his office. When I showed up he said to me, "Son, I've heard so many people around here talking about how good you are in basketball." I responded, "Coach, I'm just an average basketball player." We continued our conversation for about an hour. The word quickly spread that God had taken A.B. (Arkbar, a recent graduate) and brought him A.D., the new kid on the block. A.B. was the basketball star from the previous year. He was about 6' 4" tall and he played the point guard position. It was flattering that the coach immediately embraced my talents.

The semester went on and my ring of friends started to increase dramatically. I had become a household name within the school. Many liked me; it seemed as though everyone tried to befriend me, with the exception of other ball players interested in the same position. Along with basketball, I played junior varsity football on Thursday nights and varsity football on Friday nights during my freshmen year. Due to my athleticism in football, I was beginning to draw an overwhelming amount of attention and recognition not only from my peers but also from random people within the community.

After football season was over, the head basketball coach invited me to participate in the varsity basketball practice. This was an amazing opportunity for a freshman, yet I endured several intentional fouls from my main competition. I had become well-known for my athleticism, which was threatening and intimidating to other members of the team competing for the same position, especially Derek . The word was all around town that Coach had a new point guard on the team. Derek would trip me during fast breaks and then foul me extra hard into the posts. These rivalries made my acclimation to the team more challenging than necessary, but I worked through it.

Derek was the other potential point guard I competed against the most. Only standing 5' 10" tall, he attempted to purposely injure me on several occasions. I never let his actions discourage me because I was able to rely on my own talents and determination.

AD

Throughout my high school years at Bullock County High, I was quite the athlete. Because of my abilities in both basketball and football, I was supported and praised by my teachers, family, friends, and coaches. During a game we played against Booker T. Washington, I can remember the entire crowd chanting my name: "We want A.D. We want A.D. We want A.D." (A.D. was my nickname). The coach looked at me, started smiling, and told me to get in the game at the buzzer.

When I got in the game, the crowd relaxed. I dribbled the ball up the court and found myself in a trap, but I immediately found my way out. I then passed the ball off to the center and he slam-dunked it. Booker T. Washington stole the ball so I trailed the guy down the court and pinned the ball against the glass. The crowd went wild. For the next couple of games I held the point guard starting position and that's when my high school basketball career soared. From then on, every Friday and Tuesday night games had nearly sell-out crowds.

Just as my basketball career began to blossom, I started to experience turbulence at home. My Uncle Dubose had been beckoned to send me back to Florida to live with my parents. My mother wanted me to come back. Of course, this was completely devastating for me. If I could have had sole discretion on my life's choices, I would have stayed in Alabama, where I had spent the beginning of my life and now where I was beginning to create a name for myself. I especially didn't want to leave the various old friends I had grown up with and now the many new friends I had accumulated. I was just starting to get accustomed to high school culture in Alabama. Unfortunately, I was to succumb to my mother's wishes by making another journey to Florida to be with my parents for the summer.

As soon as I arrived in Florida that summer, I expressed my refusal to live there. Midway, Alabama was my home. It was the only place I found comfort in, the only place I felt loved, and the only place I had ever longed to be.

Thankfully, shortly after my return to Florida, my old AAU basketball coach immediately recruited me to play for him again. Since I was to permanently reside in Haines City, I began to play YBOA and AAU basketball under the leadership of Coach Milton.

To my surprise, my new teammates were all around excellent players. One of my teammates was Amare Stoudemire, who currently plays in the NBA for the Phoenix Suns. When we played together, many people compared our similarities in playing styles and physical characteristics. He was 6'5" tall and I was 6'2". He played the forward and center positions and I played the guards positions.

That year a Trucking Company sponsored the team and our team adopted the name "McClain All-Stars." As a team we practiced together, played in numerous tournaments, and actually went undefeated the entire summer. We became so good that many coaches brought their teams in to scrimmage against us. Among those teams were also international players that were visiting the state to go to the Orlando Magic camp.

Although our skills on the court were admirable, our resources were not. We may have played like we had access to the best facilities and resources, but that was a facade. For example, our transportation consisted of a van with only front driver and passenger windows. While in the van riding throughout the city from game to game we often suffered through treacherous heat, but we didn't mind. We were humble and only cared about playing basketball. Material items and opportunities to participate in extracurricular activities are luxuries that many young people often expect and take for granted, but I had to earn these opportunities. In contrast, I was expected to help pay for food and clothing and so I got a job at the Best Western Hotel where my mother was the Manager of Housekeeping. I was assigned to work in the laundry room. I worked approximately four to five days a week, which worked in my favor, because I was allowed to take off for my basketball games. I spent my money on survival necessities and saved the remainder. I adopted my grandma's tactics for saving money. She taught me to hide money underneath the mattress. Life in Florida this time around didn't seem so bad. I was able to play and flourish in the game I love, while I continued to make new friends and learn new work skills.

I had been conditioning myself to be content with my life in Florida but it took a conscious effort every day. I longed for Alabama. I was trying earnestly to convince myself to be happy and maintain stability in Florida, but with each passing day, I was becoming more and more frustrated with my living situation.

One evening I listened to a conversation that my mom and my sister Gretchen were having openly in front of me. My sister was trying to encourage my mother to let me go back to Alabama. She refused. To this day, I believe that my mother's consistent refusal was a result of the time she had lost in the earlier stages of my childhood. When reflecting on these memories, I can now understand her stubbornness then, even though it discouraged me so much growing up. At the time, I felt that her decisions about my life and well-being were completely selfish. After many discussions in regard to my residency, my mother's ultimate decision was for me to stay in Florida permanently. Again, all I could do was pray and cry. Without permission or approval, I came to the conclusion that I was leaving and never coming back.

The following morning, my mother knocked on my bedroom door to see if I was ready for work. I told her I wasn't feeling well. She said,

"Okay. I will see you later this evening." After she left for work, I immediately sought it as an opportunity to leave for Alabama without any disruptions.

I waited until she was clearly out of sight before I began to research my options for transportation. I went to the kitchen to look in the local yellow pages for the nearest Greyhound bus station. Impulsively, I decided to leave on the next bus going to Alabama. I just knew I had to leave early enough so that no one would catch up with me.

After furiously packing up my belongings and gathering my savings from underneath my mattress, I walked next door to my friend Jeremy's house and knocked on his window, seeking a ride to the bus station. Luckily, he answered, "What's going on, man?" I asked, "Can you do me a favor?" "What's up?" he replied. Anxiously, I asked, "Can you take me to the bus station?" Without hesitation he responded, "Sure, I will drop you off up there." I was officially leaving the Sunshine State on a Greyhound bus, hoping never to return. I knew my parents would begin searching for me but I made a vow that I was not going to return, regardless of their persistence.

LONG RIDE TO ALABAMA

After being dropped off at the Greyhound bus stop, I cautiously approached the counter and looked up at the nicely uniformed ticket agent. In a raspy voice, the agent asked me, "Where are you going, young man?" I hesitated for a moment and replied, "To Alabama to visit my family." Then he asked, "What city in Alabama are you going to? What's your final destination?" I was feeling edgy and tense but muttered, "I'm sorry, Sir. I'm going to Montgomery, Alabama." My feelings of nervousness began to escalate but I refused to turn back. After struggling through my feelings of anxiety and maintaining confidence in my decision, the ticket transaction was complete. When the bus finally arrived, the driver stepped outside the bus to collect ticket stubs. As I proceeded to get on the bus, I put my bags in the luggage compartment and ran up the steps. I walked down the aisle of the bus. Slowly ambling by many passengers, I noticed that some were older and some were younger. I finally claimed an empty seat toward the back. After about an hour of riding, the driver announced, "First four stops are: Orlando, Ocala, Jacksonville, and Greyhound express to Nashville, TN."

The entire trip to Alabama seemed like it was never going to end. City after city, I thought my father or someone would be waiting at each bus station to take me back to Florida. I started to look out the window into the sky, thinking about the past, present, and the future. I could see the sun folding into the clouds and the moon starting to make its first appearance for the evening. It was a beautiful symbol of my liberation. It had been a long, emotional, and draining day. But the day went on and as the trip got longer, I started to wonder whether or not anyone had been searching for me. My mind was like a broken record; I kept wondering, "If they are looking for me, where were they looking?" I was also worried that my friend might have told them that he dropped me off at the bus station. Often times, though, the thought of, "Do they even care where I am?" crossed my mind. All of these thoughts among other uncertainties ran through my mind throughout the trip like a reverberating echo.

Despite these fears I was still just as determined to make it home to Alabama.

In the midst of all my thoughts, the bus driver abruptly announced that he was planning on stopping at the next rest area where we would be for a few minutes. After getting off the bus I went to use the pay phone to give my aunt notice of my arrival.

With a few hours left in the trip, I could see that the finish line was in sight. I could taste the victory of freedom from my bus seat. I refer to my bus seat by name; I call it "16" because that was the exact amount of hours I rode in that seat on the Greyhound bus. When I finally arrived at the bus station in Montgomery, Alabama, there stood my Aunt Lizzie and her boyfriend ready to pick me up. Home sweet home!

The day after my arrival my parents found out that I was safe and sound. I refused to talk to them directly but they knew where I was and whom I was staying with. Only a few days had passed before everyone in my family found out that I left Florida for Alabama. Some members of my family started to call me the "fugitive." I wasn't very happy about leaving or even disobeying my parents, but I felt that moving back to Alabama was the best thing for me. Do I regret leaving? No. Looking back now, I believe that I made the right choice.

That school year I returned to Bullock County High School after one tough summer break. Coach Huffman and I had a conversation about my future as a high school and college athlete. Coach told me to continue making good grades, practice my basketball skills, and to stay free of trouble. He said, "Daniels, you have an extraordinary gift to play basketball. I've coached two of your uncles and one of your cousins; so, you have it in your blood line." Unrelenting, he pressed on. "The difference between you, your uncles, and cousin is that you are one of the tallest point guards I've ever coached." He started to give me advice on how to make my dream of basketball as a career start to happen. "The first thing you should do is take the

ACT and prepare for college." Confidently he stated, "I expect to have you signed with Auburn or wherever you want to go by October of your junior year." After Coach's lecture, I decided to play football for one more season and retire it as a sport in order to make my passion for basketball an absolute priority.

3RD DOWN AND 6

In the middle of my sophomore year I earned the position of running back for the football team. That year, Bullock County experienced an extensive amount of rainfall, which left the field completely saturated for weeks. Although the field was waterlogged, our season was to continue as scheduled. The next team on the schedule was against Lafayette and the field was still wet. Immediately before the start of the game, Coach Foulks advised me to put on some rain cleats because rain cleats are designed to have a strong grip in the sod. Shortly after kick-off the weather started to clear and the field became somewhat dry. The game was getting very nasty, with little action on both offense and defense. Suddenly there was a shift in momentum. Our team had made a first down. Ambitiously, the coach called a 39 toss, which is a standard play that occurs when the center hikes the ball to the quarterback who then tosses the ball to the running back.

After running toward the sideline with two defenders to beat, I maneuvered to the right, back to the left, and then planted my left foot in the ground; turning around pressing off of the defender's left shoulder. While my feet were planted in the ground, I heard a snap in my knee. I fell to the ground and grabbed my knee, screaming loudly in excruciating pain, "I think I tore my ligaments!" My knee instantly swelled up and people gathered around me while the crowd stood to their feet. The entire crowd stood there silently, awaiting word of my physical condition. After several minutes on the ground, I was taken to the sideline, where I received treatment. Aside from the many agonizing days spent seeing my grandmother suffering until she passed away, this was one of the worst days of my life.

It turned out that I had torn my anterior cruciate ligament (ACL). It's one of the most important ligaments of the knee, which helps enable twists and turns. It is also the most commonly injured knee ligament damaged by athletes. Usually the injury occurs when someone tries to rapidly change directions with the leading leg out, twisting the knee, or sudden high-pressure contact, especially from the side. Many said that my career was probably over – it's very unusual for someone to return one hundred percent after an injury like this. Unfortunately, there were many things that changed as a result of my injury. One significant change was that my friends and fans diminished. But an even more devastating change involved the end of all the talk about me being able to sign with college basketball teams such as Auburn, Alabama, Tennessee, and Duke, just to name a few. In the face of the loss of support and attention I felt that I had to come back better than before in order to prove everyone wrong. I was determined to change the negative energy into a positive, grand comeback.

That was my last year playing football. I chose not to finish out the season. Instead, I shot free throws and jumpers every day for at least four to five hours – holding a grudge against the world, against any naysayer, against the doubters, and especially against all of those who thought I wouldn't be a threat upon my return. I was determined to make it back and to take my team to a state title. One unfortunate part about being injured was that I had to return to Florida in order to have the ACL surgery because I was insured through my parents who were still living in Haines City. I didn't have health insurance that would cover me in Alabama. My aunt and uncle hadn't assumed the responsibility of insuring me because they had to take care of their own children. However, I continued to practice despite my injury – I knew that I had to stay in rhythm in order to maintain my jump shot and my sense of the game.

The summer following my sophomore year I traveled to Florida alone to see a doctor about my knee injury. My first appointment was with the family physician, Dr. Jane, who ran tests on my knee. After he ran the tests, he recommended that I see an orthopedic surgeon, Dr. Dowdy, a renowned surgeon at the hospital. I waited for several weeks before I finally got an appointment. I arrived at his office and the nurse called me to the back. Dr. Dowdy shifted my knee and asked me where the pain was. He concluded that I had torn my ACL and he was going to have to replace it with a tendon. He then scheduled a date and time for me to have an MRI to make sure there wasn't any more damage around the area. After surgery Dr. Dowdy recommended that I go to physical therapy for at least four to six months. This was a disaster for my teammates, my coaches, and me as my mother told me that I would have to stay in Florida in order for my physical therapy to be insured.

Refusing to relocate, I decided to return to Alabama, regardless of not being insured there. Fortunately, the therapist gave me an exercise sheet to take home with me. While in Alabama I followed these exercises religiously each and every night.

For months thereafter, in addition to performing my own physical therapy every day after school, I would practice free throws. Within the first couple of months of therapy, I started running and jumping with the basketball in hand. Eventually I started playing at half speed but was still cautious of my ACL. Every night I would play until around 9 p.m. or until my aunt would request that I come in. She told me that other people were trying to sleep because of work the next day. If it were up to me, I would have played all night long. I was driven by the urge to take my team to their first state title. However, I knew that if I was going to accomplish this, I had to get better.

I was slowly approaching my six-month checkup with Dr. Dowdy, which was scheduled during Christmas break. I went to his office with the hope of getting permission to play sports again. Dr. Dowdy noted that my ACL was healing properly but my range of motion still needed work. In order for a person to get the full range of motion back, it is necessary to do extensive, uncomfortable stretches. This is a painful experience, but it is necessary. Losing range of motion can result in another operation to remove scar tissue. Although Dr. Dowdy suggested that I work on my range of motion, he released me to participate in sports again.

The fate of my basketball career depended solely on Dr. Dowdy's recommendation. There was absolutely no way around it. My coach was awaiting Dr. Dowdy's permission through written documentation. Unbeknownst to my doctor, I had already begun to prepare for what would be half a basketball season. After getting proper release to play, I felt comfortable to go full speed but I knew that I wasn't prepared to compete at a high level. I returned to the team with a mission to make everyone around me better while simultaneously becoming the best leader that I could be. Although I didn't have full strength in my knee, I did have a high basketball IQ which helped me as a leader on the court.

BAD JUDGMENT TERRIBLE RESULTS

During the Christmas break in Haines City, my cousin and I spent several days playing basketball and watching television together. One particular morning, I went to the gym to play basketball and lift weights without him because he was still sore from the day before. I borrowed my cousin's jacket and my dad's truck and headed on without him. While on my way to the gym, I noticed a woman about ten yards away trying to flag me down. She was standing on the opposite side of the street waving both her arms in the air. Thinking nothing of it, I kept going. After spending about four hours at the gym, I saw the same woman again as I was heading home. She was just as eager to get my attention then, as she was earlier. Once I got to the house, I realized that I had left my cousin's jacket at the gym.

When I came in, my cousin immediately asked me where his jacket was. "I must've left it at the gym," I told him. Immediately we left for the gym. While in the truck, stopped at a red light, I saw the same woman waving vigorously. As I pointed in her direction, I stated, "Man, that woman has been trying to stop me all day." "Why didn't you stop?" he replied. "I was by myself," I answered defensively. "Why don't you see what she wants?" Curiously, I stopped the truck while my cousin rolled down the window to see what she wanted. The woman had on loose fitting jeans and a collared shirt with her hair back. As she slowly approached the truck, my cousin asked, "What do you want? Roger here says you've been trying to stop him all day." The woman replied, "You stopped. What do you want?" I quickly interjected, "Ma'am, I'm sorry. We only stopped because you have been trying to flag me down all day since this morning." She completely ignored me and initiated a conversation with my cousin. He said, "Let me talk to her for a second. Watch this." Feeling uneasy about this woman and the entire situation, I quickly said, "We need to get your jacket.

For some reason I was overcome by nervousness and discomfort. My cousin joked, "Roger, I'm just going to play around with this woman." The entire time my cousin was speaking to this woman, I was thinking of ways to lure him away from her. Jokingly I said, "This woman is an undercover police officer. Look at the shades hanging out of her pockets." He asked her, "You aren't an undercover cop are you? Let me see." As he was asking the question, he began to grab for the glasses hanging out of her pocket. I could tell that this was definitely beginning to be a bad situation to be in. "I'm about to go!" I exclaimed. As I started to back up the truck, police cars completely surrounded us. After the police had me blocked in, I turned to my cousin and shouted, "You stupid fuck! What did you do to this woman?" Exploding in laughter he said, "I was just joking with her, I was only playing around."

The police approached the truck from all angles. The officer to my left told me to put my hands on the steering wheel. Then he opened the door and asked me to get out with my hands up. I got out of the truck as he read me my rights. I asked, "What did I do?" "You should know what you did," he replied sternly. The officer searched me. He didn't find any money or identification. As I was put into the back of a police car, I noticed my cousin wasn't being treated as harshly. The arresting officer whispered to his partner, "This guy doesn't even have any money." The partner responded, "Search the entire vehicle until you find something." I overheard one of the officers mention that my cousin had made a lewd comment by asking, "How much is it for some head?" To this day I don't recall such a comment. I highly doubt my cousin would have seriously asked that, especially since neither one of us had any money. After I was put into the police car, I overheard another officer say, "The passenger was the one doing the talking, shouldn't he be taken in, too?" The officer then asked me, "Were you the driver or the passenger?" "I was driving," I replied forlornly.

The police were going to allow my cousin to walk home. "If you don't pick him up, we don't have a case," I heard an officer state. The officers then picked my cousin up and took him down to the station. We were put in a holding cell for about two hours before we were released. We walked about two miles from the police station back to the truck.

When we made it home, we explained everything to my mother, but she didn't believe us. I expected my parents to hire an attorney but they didn't. They didn't even seem nearly as concerned about this as I was. My parents were informed that the charges would be dropped; therefore, they decided not to invest in an attorney. This heinous situation turned out to be one of the most frustrating circumstances I had ever been faced with. I felt that my parents didn't do everything they could have done to make sure this incident wouldn't be on my record. I was innocent! I needed my family to support me more than anything and to my dissatisfaction, I was not receiving it. I will never forget that day or the extraneous amount of grief it caused me. I use this experience as a guide to be more careful about what I say and the company I keep. This random occurrence challenged my thoughts of the legal system, my parents, my cousin, and my ability to effectively argue my case.

LIFE OFF THE COURT

Since the eighth grade, I have lived in five different households within five school years and throughout the summers. It got to be very confusing. In eighth grade, I resided in Florida with my parents. In ninth grade, I stayed with my Uncle Dubose in Alabama, who worked as a maintenance man at a cotton mill. By 10th grade, I moved in with my Aunt Lizzie, who worked on a plantation as a housekeeper. Shortly after visiting doctor Dowdy, I moved in with my Aunt Barbara, who worked as a day care teacher. Conveniently, she had a half-court basketball court, which is mainly what kept me there.

Several times throughout high school, I would switch between my Aunt Lizzie's house and my Aunt Barbara's house in four-week intervals. Moving from house to house was easier than it sounds because my aunts only lived a mile apart and being required to wear a uniform at school meant less baggage to carry. Although there was a lot of movement and instability due to moving from location to location, one consistent thing that remained the same was Bullock County High School. Never once did I have to change schools because all the relatives that I resided with lived within the same district. Although we lived in Midway, my school in Union Springs was located 20 miles away. Regardless of which house I was staying at, many times it was difficult for me to find a ride back toward the country after a late basketball practice. I would sit at the local McDonald's in Union Springs at least twice a week after practice, sometimes waiting hours to catch a ride home. This McDonald's was located in a shopping center that also contained a Family Dollar, a Piggly Wiggly grocery store, and a movie gallery. I would eat a 99-cent double cheeseburger and then visit some of my high school friends that were employed at the Piggly Wiggly until the end of the first shift at Wayne Farm. Wayne Farm was a nearby poultry factory, which was the major employer of the residents in Midway and Union Springs. The locals referred to the factory as "The Chicken House." Several people from my neighborhood worked at the chicken house and if I was lucky, I could catch a ride home.

Catching a ride back to the country was just one of the many obstacles I had to face growing up, but it was necessary. Just like moving around from house to house wasn't fun, but it, too, was necessary for me. In addition, I can recall being told that I was a hopeless case and that I wouldn't amount to anything. Even though these words were hurtful to me, they also encouraged me to do better. I realized that they were only words from one person's perspective. At a very young age, I decided not to let other people's negative opinions define my character.

Each of the households I lived in taught me something different about life, both good and bad. However, it wasn't until my junior and senior years that I became reacquainted with a distant cousin who taught me the most valuable life-changing lessons that I still cherish today. Toward the end of my junior year of high school, I started to become increasingly intrigued by my older cousin Gregory, who was an assistant principal and practicing teacher in the elementary school, 150 yards away from my high school. Greg was the son of my Uncle Dubose, the same Uncle Dubose who had been my guardian in Alabama since my grandmother died. Greg grew up in Detroit, Michigan with his mother. Immediately after basic training for the United States Army Reserves, Greg enrolled at Auburn University in Montgomery, Alabama.

As a junior in high school subconsciously searching for guidance, I found myself once again in awe of my cousin Greg. There was something in him that was refreshing and stimulating to me. Moreover, he was the first stable and significant male role model in my life. He embraced a wider, more extensive perspective of life as a whole in comparison to people I had been surrounded by. He was well spoken and very intelligent. Greg was seven years older than me and embodied a world of knowledge, awareness, and understanding that captivated me. I started visiting him at the elementary school just to talk. Most people in Midway, including me, seemed to lack exposure to cultures outside of the town in comparison to Greg. Aside from my trips to Florida, I rarely traveled out of town because few people I knew had cars. My attitude toward Midway slowly began to change. Although it was the only place I had ever considered home, I began to develop a curiosity for more.

Greg lived 45 miles away in Montgomery and commuted to Bullock County to work every day. During the end of my junior year, after basketball season, I began to travel home with Greg, stay the night, and come back to Bullock County for school the next morning. During my visits with Greg, we would go out to eat. I was beginning to be exposed to different varieties of restaurants and environments. A lot of times he would cook and invite some of his friends. At that time he was living in an apartment complex that had a pool and a gym. We would go swimming and lift weights together. During our time spent together, Greg would talk to me as if I was his own peer but still provided me with sound advice to prepare me for important decision-making in the future. We talked about everything, from academics to basketball to my life experiences, the importance of image, respecting females, and most importantly, being reliable and hardworking. Greg became the most positive and influential male figure I had ever known. We had become so close that when I talked about him or introduced him to people, I called him my brother.

Although I was more than welcome to visit Greg anytime in Montgomery, transportation was not always guaranteed to me. Greg decided to save money by riding in a car pool with four other teachers from his school. A lot of times there wasn't enough room for me, which prevented me from having a ride to Montgomery. Since I had become accustomed to traveling to Montgomery with Greg at least four days a week, I made it my mission to find a consistent ride.

Eventually, I learned that my 10th grade music teacher, Mr. Boynton, lived in Montgomery as well, so I started to commute to Montgomery with him. He was a great man who took a strong interest in me when I had him in class, which led to the beginning of a special relationship. We got so close that I started to call him Mr. B. I began staying after school just to talk to him.

He was a very eccentric man whose taste for music and culture deviated from the average person in Bullock County. He introduced me to his world, which included his passion of jazz music along with his love for sushi and his dream of becoming a pilot. I became very fond of his eclectic lifestyle. Like Greg, Mr. B was always very honest with me. He also spoke to me as his equal while providing me with adult advice. He was a man that I admired and respected very much. Sometimes when I arrived in Montgomery, I would stay and visit with Mr. B and his wife long before I would go to Greg's house.

Being in Montgomery had become an essential part of my life. I had begun to build meaningful relationships with positive role models who provided me with a wealth of knowledge and valuable life lessons. Since I had spent so much of my time there, during my 12th grade school year, I got a job at Hardee's to rent a sharp tuxedo for my senior prom. Shortly after getting a job there, I moved in with my brother Greg.

While living with Greg, I continued to stay enrolled at Bullock County High School. My life in school seemed to be going fair. I had always thought that basketball was going to be my ticket out of Bullock County and so I hadn't devoted myself to anything else. After my injury, I realized I could be replaced at any time. I often worried that someone with equal or better skills would come and take my position along with my fan base. These fears motivated me to want to practice harder and come back stronger. Realistically, I was forced to think about other career goals aside from basketball. For the first time in my life, I was thinking about college academically and not only for basketball. I continued to maintain a B average with college in mind. Greg encouraged me to do all that I could to make it to college.

I experienced difficulties with a particular teacher my junior year. To this day, I personally feel that this teacher discriminated against student athletes, especially me. For example, whenever I would raise my hand to participate, he would purposefully ignore me. Many times, I was the only student in class attempting to participate; therefore, it felt very personal.

Furthermore, this teacher challenged my confidence and my ability because he failed to provide positive reinforcement and praise. Moreover, the course involved many rigorous assignments. Unfortunately, even after exerting a strenuous amount of effort, I failed the course. Thankfully, I was able to retake the class offered at a private school in

Montgomery. I completed the class the second time with a B, which I gladly shared with my original teacher for that class.

Throughout my life off of the court, I have learned so many lessons. And although I have been faced with challenges and adversities, I have also been blessed with friends and family who provided me with hope and assurance. At times, I felt like a failure succumbed to fall into the pit of mediocrity but I always persevered and rose above average. Often times I experienced pain that made me lose almost all my hope in achieving my dreams but through it all, I always strived for the best outcome and came out on top. As a result of my experiences, I have come to realize that I cannot control the negative things that other people think, say, or do, but I can control the way I react to it. Greg taught me to never give up and to never let anyone tell me what I can't do or what I'm not capable of being.

HYDROPLANE

One late evening after school, I asked my aunt if I could borrow her car to pick up my little cousin from basketball practice. Every now and then she would give me permission to drive her car but I didn't drive often, so I was always excited to get behind the wheel. There was a profound sense of freedom and independence I felt when I was driving. There had been cloudy skies with heavy rain the entire day, but surprisingly she said yes. After picking up my cousin, we stopped by the McDonald's drive-thru to grab some food to take back to the house. As we made our way to the main two-lane highway, I started to notice the dangers of driving in the rain. The road had accumulated a lot of water, which was beginning to flood the street. Little did I know, I was about to experience the serious consequences of driving foolishly in the rain.

Even though there was already an extensive amount of water on the road, I nonchalantly reached into the McDonald's bag for my fries and sandwich. Despite the rain I had the car in cruise control at an accelerated speed, with one hand on the steering wheel and the other inside the McDonald's bag grabbing food. All of a sudden, I heard the rain gushing against the quarter panels of the car.

I then felt a shift in the rear of the car, which caused us to hydroplane toward the right side of the road. The steering wheel got so hard to turn that I dropped the sandwich and tried to regain control of the car with both hands. Despite my efforts, the car continued to slide toward the far right side of the road and I lost all control. As we continued to slide uncontrollably to the right, we started down a steep hill backwards, hit a gate, and landed in a pond. This car was electrical with power windows and power doors. I saw my life flash before my eyes because I thought that the windows and doors would totally shut down due to the extreme amount of water entering the vehicle. My little cousin jumped out of the car while I was still inside – dazed by what happened. He kept calling my name, "Roger! Roger! Roger!" His voice sounded faint. Instantly, I became alert to the situation and replied, "Yeah! Yeah!" He said, "Man get out of the car and come to the bank of the pond." I finally snapped out of it and swam to the bank. We then climbed up the very steep hill and tried to wave someone down to help us. No one stopped, so I decided to run to the closest store to call for help. Randy stayed near the car while I walked down the road. When I left, I noticed that people were starting to stop their cars when they saw Randy, standing there desperately with his clothes tattered and drenched.

Upon my long walk along Highway 82, I finally arrived at a truck stop. I asked the clerk behind the counter if I could use the phone. He asked me if there was something wrong and I told him we had just had a bad accident up the road. I called my family to notify them of what had happened. After an hour of waiting, a tow truck came up the highway. The accident had caused most of my family to rush to the scene, too. Everyone, including Aunt Barbara, Uncle Terry, Aunt Lizzie, Uncle Dubose, Randy, myself, and the owner of the property, stood there as the car was lifted out of the water. The family decided to put the car in the shop and request a diagnostics test. The report came back to say that the car needed a new computer system because the computer on a car is the memory or brains of the car. Luckily, the car wasn't beyond repair.

Although this was a treacherous experience, I am very blessed to have been able to walk away from the accident without injury. I thank God every day for sparing my life. From that day forward I vowed to wear a seat belt as well as educate others on its importance.

BASKETBALL

After the hydroplane experience I began to view my life differently. Even to this day, I consistently drive the speed limit and follow all the laws of the road. I was able to come to the realization that life is a blessing and I must not take it for granted. Therefore I began to embrace each day, each gift I possessed, and each talent, especially basketball.

Despite my previous knee injury, I entered into my senior year with the state championship in mind. The state title was the prize. With my eye on the prize, I dedicated myself as the team's leader; one who would help cultivate and educate the team on unity and collaboration. I realized early on that just because we were a group of people with a common purpose, we did not necessarily constitute an effective team. In order to win the state championship, I firmly believed that each player must unilaterally conduct tasks high in complexity with many interdependent subtasks. I have always believed that motivation is the key ingredient for success in any team or organization. A person can have all of the technical skills in the world; however, if he can't motivate his team, he will not achieve success. As a team leader, I took the responsibility of motivating my teammates to succeed to their best potential.

I motivated my team through effective communication along with my basketball skills and technique in order to be an asset to the team both physically and mentally. Because my knee was still slightly weak, I emphasized communication as the foundation of successful teamwork. I learned that in order to work together effectively, team members must be aware of the team's vision, mission, purpose, specific goals, and allocated roles and responsibilities. I maintained ongoing review, evaluation, and feedback to facilitate such teamwork.

It is often said that leaders are born and not made. The truth is, several factors contribute to the development of a leader. It was my senior year of basketball that helped contribute to my development as a leader along with my ability to empathize with the needs of the people being led.

Basketball was always the number one love in my life but unfortunately I knew I could no longer play hard nor could I continue to rely on basketball as a career. My injury forced me to look into other avenues and helped me to highlight my other strengths and talents.

The team began to bond. Every member started to contribute to the overall purpose of the season. Although I proved to be an effective facilitator who helped my teammates to identify their unique abilities and talents, I was working very hard to restore my place physically on the basketball court. After school I would lift weights, strength train, practice free throws, and run three miles a day to secure my place on the team.

My leadership led the team to improve drastically in contrast to how they had been playing without me for the past two seasons. One season during my absence, the team won 14 games and lost 16. Unfortunately, they also lost the first game of the area tournament. When I returned to the team, I was determined to help us go all the way. I had great expectations for us as a team and for my last season at Bullock County High School.

Being the team leader involved an immense amount of pressure along with strengthening and improving my skills. I was also beginning to worry about my life after high school. Playing college basketball was something that I had always entertained; however, my coach often reminded me of my knee injury and began to encourage me to consider other avenues. This was very disheartening because basketball was my love, my passion, my life – yet I could foresee it coming to an end. I held on to it tightly even though I knew my opportunity to play college or pro ball ended when I tore my ACL.

That season ended with a record of 24 wins and only 3 losses. After our 15th win, my coach predicted that we could definitely win the tournament. We were able to host the area tournament and win, which was an honor because only the teams with the best record are qualified to host an area tournament. After winning the area tournament, we continued on to the regional tournament held at Troy State University.

We were very excited about meeting this great milestone but we were still hungry for the state championship. We went into the first round of the tournament with a good attitude, high energy, and our eyes set on the trophy. Shortly after the start of the game, we were leading by 10 points. By halftime we were in hot pursuit of winning the first game of the tournament. Once we got into the locker room to debrief the first half, Coach indicated that there were scouts in the audience. I was very confident that my ability to lead and play would impress the scouts.

We started the second half of the game with just as much enthusiasm and drive for the win, but I believe that the majority of the team felt pressure to play well individually due to the presence of the scouts. We had allowed the presence of scouts in the stands to distract us from playing together as a unified team. My teammates started shooting the ball every time it was passed to them. Regretfully, we ended up losing focus and we lost the game by about 10 points. After the game I walked over to the other team and shook their hands and congratulated them on a job well done. This moment was very difficult to deal with, mainly due to how we lost the game. We didn't play together as we should have. It was a team effort that got us there but we didn't embrace this effort once we made it to the regional tournament.

When we got on the bus to head back to school I went to the last seat and stayed there for the rest of the night. The ride back to Bullock County was extremely long, quiet, and emotional for many of us. I looked out the window with my head held high, trying to leave everything on the court. I looked into the wilderness, daydreaming about what could've been. A tear drifted from my eye, slowly coasted down my cheek and eventually evaporated below my chin – this was a tear of sorrow and defeat. I couldn't stop thinking about my previous goal of winning the state tournament but it finally sunk in: there was no tomorrow, no next game, or next year to redeem ourselves. My career as a high school basketball player was officially over.

From that day forward I vowed to never allow my teammates to lose focus again. Days after the devastating loss, I called a meeting with some of the returning players. I talked to them about dedication, no matter the circumstances. I told them, "It will be the team that will take you to the mountaintop. There's no one individual that can win the game by himself. You have to bond like brothers, starting today. You must connect well before the season begins. You have to understand each other's strengths and weaknesses." It was important for me to emphasize that although we had made it to the playoffs with a fairly decent record, we didn't win because we didn't stick together. "You guys in this next season have a chance to make history. I will be in college next year, but while I will not be on this team, I have absolute confidence in you guys. So if you guys want to make a championship run next year, you must start preparing today." I left the team with words of inspiration in hopes that their individual egos would not destroy the team's goals.

HEADING TO COLLEGE

As graduation came near, I began to think about what college I could attend that would allow me to play basketball. I only had options of playing basketball at a junior college level as opposed to the ideal four-year institution. Following the basketball season I continued to work hard by lifting weights, shooting free throws, and running. I was practicing hard to get ready for basketball wherever I ended up after high school. I overheard several students talk about the colleges or universities they planned to attend, which made me feel slightly insignificant because I didn't have a substantial plan for college yet. Upon my high school graduation, I still didn't have a plan for my future.

My indecisiveness led me to feel very confused, particularly when Greg would frequently ask me about my plans following graduation. I usually replied with "the military" but I really didn't have a plan. Greg was persistent in initiating conversations about my future. I discovered that he wouldn't accept the military as my answer and continued to ask me about my future until I provided a substantial plan with details. I have always respected and admired Greg, so I wanted to make a meaningful decision about my life that would make him proud. After all, he received a higher education and he came from an even more unstable background than I did. He was an inspiration to me and I hated not having an answer for him. He had high expectations for me, even when I didn't have them for myself. He believed in me and saw the potential that I couldn't. He was able to communicate the perfect words in order to motivate me in ways that led me to feel confident in myself. On graduation night my family and friends arrived to cheer me on. I can especially remember Greg congratulating me on meeting this tremendous milestone. Greg's presence at my graduation was more meaningful to me than anything. Throughout my life he has proved to be someone I could rely on and trust even with my deepest insecurities.

Weeks after graduation, I still hadn't reached a decision about my future. Greg insisted that I was too smart for the military and I was starting to notice that people who graduated with lower grade point averages were getting accepted into college; therefore, I was starting to consider college even more. When I felt secure about college, I immediately told Greg. Eagerly he said, "Let's make it happen." Without delay, we requested an application and financial aid information from Alabama

A&M University. After completing and sending off the application, we anxiously anticipated the answer. I received a response by mail within five weeks. Apprehensively, I clutched the envelope. To my surprise, I was accepted! Greg and I celebrated.

With my latest and exciting news, I called my cousin Bisharrah to inquire about her plans for college. Coincidentally, Bisharrah and I were accepted into the same school for the fall semester. We made arrangements to attend the freshman orientation together since we were both from the Union Springs area traveling north to Huntsville. The idea of leaving Midway and going to college was a new and exciting transition in my life, and I was pleased to share this experience with my cousin.

We left Union Springs at five in the morning and arrived in Huntsville at the Alabama A&M University campus three hours later. I was amazed to see how drastically different Huntsville was in comparison to Midway, Union Springs, and even Montgomery. There were so many large buildings and friendly people from all over the country. I was thrilled and overwhelmingly excited by the new culture shock that Huntsville provided.

During the orientation, I took time to speak with the university's assistant basketball coach, Coach Hayes, in order to share with him my previous experience as well as express my interest in the basketball program. He showed an interest in me as well. He requested video images of me playing basketball in order to aid in the determination process, and encouraged me to tryout for the team during the spring semester.

I couldn't wait to start a new life and assimilate into this new environment. Fortunately, the university required that all prospective freshmen spend an entire week on campus through a program called Operation Jump Start. This program took place a month after orientation. My cousin Edward was also attending Alabama A&M University that fall so we decided to ride together and later room together on campus. After attending Operation Jump Start, I was more than excited to live on campus and experience the college life.

My first week of college was spent unpacking, cleaning, and becoming acclimated to the area. I kept in touch with family back home through calling cards. Surprisingly, during the first week of college, I received a call from my brother Greg. It was so good to hear from him. He had worked so hard to help me discover my path along with helping me get there. He was very proud to see his commitment to me and my future become a reality. During that phone conversation, Greg continued to motivate me as usual. He said, "Roger, you have been granted an opportunity to better your life. Take advantage of this moment and understand that some folks expect you to fail or even expect you to come back home without a degree. You have to prove them wrong! It's up to you now, what are you going to do?" After listening to his lecture, I was even more confident and determined to do my best throughout college.

Greg's inspirational lectures were reflected in my grades and although Greg was proud of all I had achieved in college thus far, he wanted to ensure that I continued to prosper; therefore, he proposed a challenge. He told me that if I made the honor roll my first semester, he would give me his Jeep. I worked extremely hard during that semester and finished with a high GPA. During Christmas break, I went back to Montgomery to visit Greg.

When I arrived home I presented my report card to Greg. "Job well done!" he responded. Then he added, "I told you that you could do whatever you set your mind to." I had expected to receive the keys to my new jeep soon after, but the entire Christmas break passed by and I still hadn't received them.

I kept assuming that Greg would remember to give me the keys before I left, but I was starting to realize that I may not get it at all because we hadn't even discussed the title or insurance. I finally asked him about the jeep and to my dismay he admitted, "I just wanted to prove to you that you have always been capable of doing anything you set your mind to." He continued, "This lesson should let you know that you can make things happen. You don't need an incentive to do something to help your future. You have a chance to possibly live a comfortable life by obtaining a degree."

I arrived back to school without my jeep but with the same amount of determination to strive for the best grades. I was excited to be back. It was the spring semester and I was still interested in trying out for the basketball team as Coach Hayes had previously suggested. But unfortunately, due to Proposition 48, I didn't qualify to play basketball with the university. My application to the National Collegiate Athletic Association (NCAA) clearinghouse was incomplete. Therefore, I wasn't granted clearance to play sports my first year of college. As a result, I began to play intramurals in order to condition for the spring practice. I continued to play intramurals until I attempted to dunk on two guys who stood about 6'2" and 6'0" tall. In my attempt to dunk, I twisted my ankle badly.

Once again I was experiencing another injury without insurance, which created a barrier that kept me from playing basketball. With basketball tryouts steadily approaching, I had to do something really fast. I resorted to a remedy that I had once overheard Grandma recommend to my uncle when I was a child. It was a concoction of red clay and vinegar that served as a cast, which held my ankle in place and decreased the swelling. The pain continued even after a couple weeks of treatment but I was determined to tryout during the spring practice. I contacted Coach Haynes, who suggested that I go see a doctor before trying out. I made an appointment to see an orthopedic surgeon and he recommended therapy. I went to therapy for five weeks, which caused me to miss basketball tryouts. This was an unfortunate loss that disappointed me very much, so I decided to try football again.

When summer school started I decided to go down to the field house to talk to the football coach, Coach Jones. I informed him of my interest in football. After my meeting with Coach Jones, I began my strength training with Coach Hester, the strength and conditioning coach. In the mornings, we would lift weights and in the afternoons we ran wind sprints. Football practice was relatively far from my dorm; therefore, during that summer, I used some of my student loan money to purchase an inexpensive car, which definitely helped me get from the field house to my on-campus apartment. With reliable transportation, I was able to commit myself to football practice and training.

I continued to practice every day. Some days the sun was blistering hot at its highest peak. Sometimes I felt the urge to quit but I didn't give up. As the summer went on, I continued to practice. All the exposure to football allowed me to become even more compelled to play for the university. I had my mind set on playing football until the accident.

One particularly rainy day I was on my way back to campus when a car collided with mine – a woman t-boned me. My car spun around completely then struck a pole at full speed. Unfortunately, this accident was the cause of another injury. I immediately began to experience sharp lower back pains. This excruciating pain occurred mostly at night, which disturbed me while I slept. I had to see a chiropractor for several months. Once again, this was another barrier that hindered me from playing sports. I don't like to give up, but I decided that playing sports was probably not for me anymore. I gave myself a couple of weeks to think about it before making a decision. I asked God to show me the signs and guide me in the direction that he would like for me to go. After weeks of thinking, I decided to give sports up and pay more attention to academics.

In addition to all the injuries, rehabilitation, and practice, I was also fortunate enough to meet a very nice, mild tone young lady, Tanya, who reminded me a lot of my grandmother. She was very supportive of my dreams of being a college athlete, and pursing a career in education. That summer we became friends and grew closer to each other. By the end of the summer, we pursued a relationship and she became my girlfriend.

PURSUIT OF ACCEPTANCE

My interests began to extend beyond the realm of sports. I started to make new friends and become affiliated with new social networks. In January a friend of mine, named Justin Hill, invited me to attend an interest meeting hosted by the men of Kappa Alpha Psi Fraternity, Inc. These exceptional young men were looking for new recruits for their organization. I eagerly welcomed Justin's invitation because I had been actively searching for a fraternity.

After speaking with Justin, I began to inquire more about the Kappa Alpha Psi Fraternity. I heard a lot of stereotypes and generalizations, such as the Kappa's didn't accept sophomores. I had also been told that in order to qualify, one must have family members who were accepted first. It was known that people who were accepted into the fraternity were also well-known throughout the university prior to becoming a member. Members must have at least a 2.5 grade point average in order to be considered. After hearing these stories, I began to question my ability to meet the requirements. I also began to feel somewhat inadequate; however, that didn't last very long because I have never given up on anything before trying it.

The meeting was hosted one evening in the Bibb Graves building on campus. I felt anxious as I walked into the auditorium. There were hundreds of young men inside, including both members and prospective members. I noticed that the men sitting to the left were already members while the young men sitting on the right were prospective members, like me. The room was cool, yet a comfortable temperature. I could feel the eyes of hundreds of people upon me as I entered the room. Although I could hear faint voices coming from the member side, the non-member side was so silent that I could hear the wooden floor crack beneath me as I tried to locate a seat. I was conscientious of who I made eye contact with while staying attentive to how I was being perceived. I didn't want to look insecure yet I didn't want to appear arrogant; therefore, I tried my best to just blend in with the crowd rather than highlight my individual characteristics through my words or actions. I took a seat in the front row where I had a perfect view of the podium placed on the center of the stage.

Shortly after I took my seat, the young men within the room came to order and took their seats quietly in anticipation for the program to begin. There were several current and veteran members who had come to welcome us and explain the organization's values and goals.

However, there was one speaker who still sticks out to me today. Mr. Washington was the designated keynote speaker who stated, "Kappa seeks no man." Then he said, "Many are interested but only few are chosen." These words ignited my desire to be a chosen member because his message indicated to me that one must be a very special person in order to belong to such a prestigious organization.

As the program continued, Mr. Sims, the organization's advisor, proceeded to explain the application process. I listened intently and took notes as he explained the range of strenuous requirements one must obtain in order to be acknowledged or even considered for the organization. I wanted to belong so badly. Aside from my stint with football and my passion for basketball, I had discovered that I wanted to be a Kappa more than anything while attending this university. I learned that the organization was very civically involved while its standards helped to exemplify quality characteristics within individuals. Its mission statement represented everything I wanted to embody for myself.

After attending the meeting and listening to the advisors speak, I was thoroughly intrigued by the requirements of being a member. The fraternity expected maturity and dedication. Maturity to them was more than just age but a person's ability to sacrifice, set goals, show consideration, sustain an emotional balance, develop social skills, embrace intellectual competence, and display moral rectitude. A dedicated Kappa must apply this maturity to a lifelong program of action. I was pleased to discover that the men hosting the meeting were not engrossed in simple accumulation of numbers for their organization, but were more concerned about the quality and integrity of its' members.

Following the meeting, I immediately began gathering all required documents to be attached with the application in order to be considered for an interview. While turning in my information, I was surprised to hear Mr. Dennis Howell, the co-advisor of the fraternity, wish me luck during the deliberation process. Over the next few days, I waited anxiously for a response. I wondered about my results as each day passed. It was the most nerve-racking yet exciting 45 days of waiting. Finally, my eagerness and anticipation were put to ease one calm evening. It was a Sunday at 6 p.m. when I received a phone call from Mr. Sims, the organization's advisor. He called to inform me that I had been chosen for an interview with three chapter officers of Kappa Alpha Psi Fraternity, Inc.

The interview took place within the Bibb Graves building where the initial interest meeting had been held. The officers occupied two separate classrooms within the building during the interview process. One classroom was designated as a waiting room where all of the selected interviewees awaited their turn. The other classroom was designated as the actual interview location. I had prepared for this moment since that call on Sunday evening with the hopes of being accepted into the intake process, which involved studying the history and specific details of the organization and taking an exam. I said a prayer prior to the interview. I wore a brown pinstriped suit to ward off any possible critique of my appearance and professionalism. There I sat among 50 to 60 other young men, also awaiting their individual interviews.

Finally, I was called into my interview where I was asked a series of questions in regard to my intentions, my strengths, and my qualifications. I was slightly nervous, but I answered each question assertively and diligently. One of the chapter officers commented on my suit by stating, "That's a nice suit." I accepted the compliment graciously by replying with a simple, "Thank you." At the closing of the interview, I took the opportunity to thank them for their time and consideration. I also emphasized my extreme interest in the organization along with how its values coincided with my own. I shook each advisor's hand firmly and then walked out.

One week later, I received a phone call to meet in the auditorium of the Bibb Graves building. I entered the auditorium along with twenty other casually dressed young men. We had come directly from class to this meeting. It was then we learned that we had been chosen for the intake process. Mr. Waylon Sims stood before us to announce our acceptance. He stated, "All of you are among the elite. You have been chosen for the intake process. Do you accept the invitation?" He further explained the additional classes we had to take along with our registered college courses in order to prepare for membership. The classes were set up to help us prepare for the test.

To be one of the few selected from the collection of candidates to become a member of the fraternity was definitely a blessing and an honor. However, in order to be a part of Kappa Alpha Psi, we were required to take a test that assessed our ability to identify the information we had learned throughout the interview process. Fortunately, we all passed the test and were exhilarated to be presented at the Probate Show. A Probate Show is a public induction of new members – it is a moment of ceremonious celebration toward which we had all worked so hard.

The Probate Show took place on April 11, 2003, directly after spring break. I woke up early that morning in preparation for the big show. In anticipation for the day, I proudly dressed in synchronization with my line brothers by wearing brown shoes with a matching belt, khaki pants, a white button-down dress shirt, a red bow tie, and dark tinted sunglasses, all covered by a red velvet cloak with an oversized hood. I met my line brothers, one of which became my best friend, Johnnie Irby, behind Foster Dormitory on the east side of campus. On that sunny morning, we marched from the dormitory; following directly behind the veteran Kappa's who were escorted by limousine. As we marched we chanted in unison one of the various rhythmic phrases we had learned during probate practice.

After a quarter mile of marching in the street, we stopped abruptly in front of our organization's stone, diagonal from the Ralph Lee Student Center. The local police had graciously secured and blocked the street while helping to direct traffic and control the crowd. This was an exciting moment for my line brothers and me. It was an electrifying annual event that many people on campus looked forward to. The crowd contained thousands of people – students, parents, faculty members, other fraternity and sorority organization members, and even some locals. I could hear people screaming and shouting in exuberance. I could see people with balloons, bouquets of flowers, Kappa t-shirts, cards, and colorful signs. The people in the crowd were so elated and they expressed it through deep bellows of laughter, chanting, clapping, shouting, and by wearing big toothy smiles. The energy from the crowd ignited the flames within the entire line, giving us spirit and vigor. Then my appearance was revealed. I was officially welcomed as a Kappa member.

SENTIMENT

After pledging Kappa, I was able to meet some amazing, brilliant, and talented young men with similar aspirations and passions. Even today, I continue to maintain very close relationships with these exceptional men. These men are exceptional in every sense of the word by being intellectually gifted as well as being physically and mentally sharp. I am honored to have friends who are candid, linguistically articulate, sophisticated, and debonair. These men are like brothers to me and I would do anything that I could to help each and every one of them. Becoming a Kappa didn't help me make friends; it helped me establish a new family. Being a part of this fraternity has had an amazing impact on me.

Being admitted into the Kappa Alpha Psi Fraternity, Inc. was one of the greatest blessings I had ever received because I was able

95

to develop valuable relationships through the organization. This comradery allowed me to become emotionally involved with people who weren't apart of my blood lineage. These expressions of sentiment did not come naturally for me because it was not typical behavior that was regularly portrayed in any environment that I had resided in growing up. Instead, I experienced an absence of affection after my grandmother died.

My grandmother provided me with so much love. She consistently demonstrated benevolence, compassion, comfort and good will, which nourished my soul and nurtured my spirit. Since she passed, I haven't felt that kind of love again. No one in my life has been able to super cede her affection, demeanor, and warmth. I have spent my life searching to fill that void, searching to gain that same sense of comfort again, and trying to endure the same blissful sensation of nostalgic memories. To this day, I still struggle with showing and expressing emotion. However, there have been times when I have been able to identify my deep seeded emotions through the lyrics in certain songs.

One song in particular is Marvin Sap's, "I Made It." Whenever I hear this song, my eyes weld up with tears of joy, hope, and gratitude. In the song Marvin recognizes that God is always present and that all things are possible with the strength and wisdom of the all knowing and all mighty Lord. It is a beautiful song that reminds me of my life and my struggles. In the song, Marvin asserts that he too is stronger, wiser, and better with the guidance and grace of God. I never would have made it to where I am now without God. Because of my grandmother's faith and guidance, I have always put God first. I pray in the morning when I rise, before every meal, and at night before I rest. I have been astonished by the power of prayer. For example, I prayed to get out of Florida, and through God's guidance I was able to get out when I asked him to show me the way.

Another song that strikes an emotional chord within me is, "Heaven", by Jamie Foxx, which was written as a testament of his love and devotion to his grandmother; something that we both share. In the song he describes her as an angel and a person who supported his life and dreams. At times I feel that my grandmother is watching over me. I believe that her spirit is always with me. She has a hand in all of my successes and achievements. Therefore, with her by my side, I continue to strive for my best. "Heaven" is a beautiful song, which fills me with emotions of bittersweet sorrow of once having been acquainted with such a wonderful human being in person, but now being filled with her beautiful spirit. When listening to this song, I am taken to a place and time when I once felt unconditional encouragement for my personal growth and development in this world.

These songs help me to revive the strong sentiment I once felt for the truest love of my life – my grandmother. Although, I was struck with grief by the loss of her at such a young age, I haven't fully lost nor have I fully retained the idea of love. However, even as an adult, I struggle with identifying the feeling of love. Aside from my grandmother, Greg, my brother, is one of the few people I have said those three powerful words to, other than my little cousins and nephew.

I have also expressed my love to my girlfriend. Her support and love helped me make important decisions in my life. I was able to bounce ideas off of her and trust her opinion on significant issues. Without her affection and encouragement I would not be the person I am today.

I have experienced that although love is a relatively simple emotion that most people express very easily, I find it to be more complicated. Love in my mind is very powerful and sacred. Attached with the word love is responsibility and devotion. It is not a word that can be used in vain. The truest definition of love is presented in the Bible in 1st Corinthians 13:4:

Love is patient and kind. Love is not jealous or boastful; it is not arrogant or rude. Love does not insist on its own way; it is not irritable or resentful; it does not rejoice at wrong, but rejoices in right. Love bears all things, believes all things, hopes all things, and endures all things. Love never ends.

According to the content and meaning of this definition, the people who have sincerely and consistently exhibited true love in my life have been my sweet grandmother, Mrs. Willie Mae Dubose, my family, my girlfriend, and my friends who have demonstrated a nearly unattainably high standard and expectation of what I think love should be. Because of this high standard and expectation, I struggle with saying it. Although, I find love to be a valuable and sacred feeling, I find that I have the natural ability to build and maintain meaningful lifelong relationships.

Throughout my life and experiences with building and maintaining relationships, I have learned that people have an innate desire to feel valued, appreciated, worthy, and welcomed by others. Therefore, I've learned that in order to relate to others in a meaningful way, I must genuinely identify with and understand their feelings or difficulties.

One way that I demonstrate empathy is by blessing others through random acts of kindness while teaching them to do the same. For example, I allowed a friend to stay in my apartment because he wasn't awarded enough money to pay for a dorm room. I also demonstrate empathy by providing motivational messages to nearly everyone I come into contact with. People are motivated most when they know someone else believes in them. When the words, "I believe in you," are expressed to another, their previous feelings of doubt or hopelessness can be transformed into confidence, which inherently helps people turn their dreams into reality. I am driven by helping others pursue their highest potential and reaching their truest dreams and beyond.

Due to my devotion to others, I have built numerous resilient and valuable relationships with many throughout the nation. I have friends in almost every state in the nation, which came primarily due to my travels as the NEA Student Program Chairperson. But it was in my home state of Alabama where I made a lifelong kinship of new friends. While attending Alabama A&M University, I met some of the most incredible people, whom I whole-heartedly embrace today. I was fortunate to harness wonderful relationships with some of the best faculty in the nation. Many members of the faculty and staff helped to shape my character by providing me with opportunities. Some of my professors posed as pseudo parents who treated me with the same reverence as they would their own children, which made me feel that Alabama A&M University was my home away from home.

My experience at Alabama A&M University helped to mold me professionally by providing me with the skills to bestow a strong commitment and emphasis to public service. My dedication to public service was initially incorporated by extending myself to my superiors outside of the classroom, whereby I expressed my gratitude for their kindness and guidance through services such as cutting grass, helping to set up and decorate their Christmas tree, and even helping to remove brush and rubble by tractor. Although, I extended myself to their needs as much as possible, I believe that no amount of money or labor can compensate for the life lessons, skills, and opportunities that were provided to me. These lessons helped to prepare me for the greatest milestones and challenges throughout my life. With a strong support system and network base, I felt prepared to face any challenge presented before me.

STUDENT ALABAMA EDUCATION ASSOCIATION

One initial challenge I faced was choosing education as my major. Many questioned my reasoning why I chose such an unprofitable profession. However, I felt that it was one of the few ways that I could give back to my community and truly make a difference. Since my basketball and football careers were over, along with my chance to go professional, I knew I could effectively reach out to the youth through education. In the beginning, I was constantly reminded by many that I would not make a lot of money in education. Reverently, I always gave the same response, "It's not about the money – it's about having an impact." To me, giving children and young adults effective inspiration and motivation and witnessing the positive results will be more rewarding than meaningless material possessions.

I believe every child, regardless of their background, should have someone to inspire, encourage and motivate them. This is what got me to college and this is what's going to help me survive in the world. Kids are brought into this world through no fault of their own and deserve someone to guide them to success. Had it not been for Gregory, there is no way I would have filled out my college and financial aid applications. I was motivated by his ability to inspire. More importantly, he believed in me even when I doubted myself. Every child should have that same opportunity. This is why I intend to be the voice for the young and impressionable. I have dedicated the rest of my life to ensuring that the youth are inspired to identify their dreams and make them a reality.

While enrolled in the Elementary Education program, I realized the strong force within me to be a leader; however, it wasn't until my sophomore year that I was presented with an opportunity that would soon change my life and perspective forever. In order to take my practicum and participate in student teaching, I joined the Student Alabama Education Association Program for liability purposes. Initially, I didn't know much about the organization…. this would soon change.

I learned that the program is a professional organization for education majors attending a University in Alabama, whose mission is to help aspiring educators develop, understand and appreciate the teaching profession. The organization also helps college students develop leadership and professional attitudes. I would later learn that this organization would take me far in life. During my sophomore year,

I saw an advertisement for a free field trip for education majors and members of the Student Alabama Education Association. The words "free" and "trip" were immediately alluring to me. After inquiring about the details and discovering that it was a free trip to the beach, I signed up immediately. I went on this mystery trip without any expectations. I was one of many college students seeking a degree in education who attend this conference.

The opening night of the conference I met a young, petit, yet assertive woman named Dawn Sheppard who was the Chairperson of the National Education Association Student Program (NEA-SP). She demonstrated an impressive sense of enthusiasm for the NEA-SP and explained in great detail the benefits of being a leader.

After speaking with Dawn for quite some time, I shared with her my goals and passion for strengthening and influencing the youth through education. She became very adamant in advising me to become actively involved – not only in the Student Alabama Education Association, but with the National Education Association as well. She continued to explain the procedure for running for office along with the major roles and responsibilities attached to the position.

I was very impressed by her vernacular and ability to articulate her passion for the National Education Association. She was very knowledgeable about the association and issues within the public school system across the nation, and had great insight about being an effective leader. I was convinced that I had the God-given talent, passion, and ability to pursue a similar leadership role.

During the conference I decided to run as a write-in for Second Vice President – and won! Fellow peers, colleagues, and faculty at A&M were very pleased with the results. As an official elected officer for the SAEA (Student Alabama Education Association), I was granted the privilege to be a member of the state board as well as attend the National Education Association Student Leadership Conference (NEA-SLC), held in Washington D.C.

While attending the conference, I discovered there were vacancies for offices on the national level. Fortunately, these positions wouldn't interfere with school or my position as Second Vice-President of SAEA. Therefore, without hesitation, I ran as a write-in for the Resolutions Committee – a committee within the NEA that primarily focuses on organization.

Although I was undertaking new major leadership roles with new major responsibilities, I was managing my academics and fraternity responsibilities successfully. Moreover, during my term as Second Vice-President, I helped to increase membership of the SAEA both locally and statewide. I was proud of my accomplishments and was certain that I could be even more effective. As my term came to an end for Second Vice-President, I immediately decided to run for President of the SAEA. There was one candidate for President before I declared my candidacy, but after I announced my entry, my one opponent dropped out of the race and ran for Vice President instead. Ultimately, I won the election by acclamation! I won through default owing to a lack of opposition.

My vision for the program was to promote benefits for student members to embrace. In order to get started on promoting these core values, I contacted the School of Education at universities throughout the state of Alabama and expressed my visions for the program. I emphasized that SAEA was a very strong student organization with a lot to offer, including leadership, professional development, and community outreach.

Most of the college administrators were impressed with all of the benefits that the organization had to offer. Many of them were so impressed with what I presented to them that they referred me to their staff. I sat down and met with active members on campus, creating new networks and providing information to students about the conferences and various other opportunities. I worked diligently in organizing a stronger, more effective student union for education throughout Alabama.

My first major task as President occurred on April 14, 2005 when the Alabama Supreme Court made a decision to make Alabama teachers take a licensure exam to measure teaching competency. The content knowledge test, Praxis II, was decided upon and would be required in order to receive an official teaching certificate. In addition to this decision, the courts also stated that there must to be a pilot program for this test before they could adopt standard scores. Therefore, the State Board decided that they would start collecting data from the class of 2005. This decision put added stress and pressure on graduating seniors who weren't prepared for such an examination including myself.

This class had only two weeks left in school before graduation. After the final decisions had been brought to my attention, I felt that the decision was unjust for the entire class of 2005. I believed it was an unethical decision to arbitrarily mandate this on these students. My frustrations prompted and compelled me to write letters to the State Department of Education on behalf of the SAEA. Students all over the state were disgruntled and aggravated, not just because of the test, but also because of the mandatory $150.00 fee. I did everything in my power to overturn this discouraging decision.

Letter to the State Superintendent

Dr. Morton:

My name is Anthony Daniels. I am the incoming President for the Student Alabama Education Association. I am writing this letter to express my deep concern and the concern of other education majors across the state, about the recent vote of the State Department of Education to REQUIRE students who are graduating in May to take the Praxis II exam in June. Although neither I, nor any of the other students have a problem with taking the exam, but the timing could not have been more inappropriate or unfair. The students who are graduating, have made countless plans for the summer, budgets have been strained to the max preparing for graduation and paying all other fees that are required of us. We have previous obligations with summer jobs, internships, and vacations.

I have received countless emails and letters in regards to the decision that was made by the State Department of Education. I am in support of finding ways to better the future of our growing children and the leadership and capabilities of their teachers; however requiring this test with so short a notice with registration and fees to take the test due by May 10, 2005, just days before some graduate is extremely stressful and very unfair. Although the test is only for data compilation the ability to perform at one's best is reduced greatly due to time constraints and financial woes. Also, depending on performance, this could affect the ability of our graduates to get teaching positions outside of Alabama. This would not have been an issue had we had more time to prepare. I would think that in order to get the best possible scores, you would want scores from students who were well prepared and less stressed to draw from.

As a senior this affects not only my future plans but the plans of many graduating seniors across Alabama. Therefore, I am requesting that the test not be required for those students graduating in May, but perhaps the students graduating in December. The scores will be better because of the additional time to prepare, not only mentally, but physically as well.

Sincerely,

Anthony Daniels Jr.

During the summer, I attended the annual Student Leadership Conference and the National Education Association – Representative Assembly for my second time. This time the conferences were held in Los Angeles, California. Again, there were vacant offices for the National Education Association. These positions were intriguing to me, but I wanted to continue my focus on making the state of Alabama stronger than ever. Many of my colleagues and fellow peers convinced me to run for the office of Board of Directors. After numerous discussions in regard to the Board of Directors position, I was convinced that running for this office wouldn't interfere with my presidency within the SAEA.

Again I ran as a write-in. I declared my candidacy a couple of hours before the candidates' speeches.

I was the only write-in candidate on the ballot. There were about six candidates, but only three slots to be filled. After the results were reported, the Elections Chair reported that although two of the three positions were filled, one position was not. The Elections Chair also reported that two candidates would compete in a run-off. These candidates included me, and Lindsey Hewitt. Although, my chances were great, unfortunately many of the Alabama delegates weren't present and I lost the election. Even though I lost, it was a great learning experience, and more importantly, as SAEA's President, I was still determined to strengthen membership and activeness throughout the state of Alabama.

STRENGTHENING SAEA

During my presidency, my goal was to get more participants at the conferences. Another goal was to get more schools throughout Alabama involved in SAEA. As a leader of SAEA, I decided to build on the strengths and focus on the weaknesses. During my tenure, I found that the number one weakness of the organization was inactive members. Due to the lack of participation; I supremely emphasized increasing student membership and leadership development.

After conversing with various deans throughout the state of Alabama, I found a more effective approach by reaching out to students directly. Therefore, I shifted my focus away from the deans and directly targeted the education majors. This approach was extremely effective.

While communicating and reaching out to students across the state, I learned that many students were inconvenienced by the Praxis

II requirement. As an association, we made a collective decision to offer Praxis II workshops during our state conference. In addition to providing preparation for the test, the workshops helped us promote the strong values of professional development and teamwork. Members of SAEA were starting to appreciate the many benefits of the association opposed to their previous intentions of being a member strictly to receive liability coverage. As more and more prospective educators began to reap the benefits of gaining professional and leadership skills, as well as building relationships and earning privileges, the number of active members grew at our conferences. Not only was membership increasing drastically throughout the state, but non-active members became active. Many people were acknowledging our efforts in influencing this great change.

That August, I received a phone call from Jennifer Rogers, the current Chairperson of the National Education Association Student Program. She proposed that I become a member of the Advisory Committee of Student Members. This particular committee has the responsibility of making recommendations to the National Education Association Board of Directors. Although, I was intrigued by the request, I was apprehensive about taking on another responsibility, so I replied by saying, "I'm really interested in focusing on my state association and making it stronger." She remained very persistent in the matter and insisted that the position would not interfere with my duties.

I remained hesitant about accepting the position. However, the thought of being appointed to the Advisory Committee lingered on my mind. After much contemplation, I sought advisement from the state student organizer, Sandra Jackson, who indicated that taking the position would be an even greater opportunity for me and even more so for the state of Alabama. Taking the position would give me a seat with the National Education Association, whereby, the NEA would then provide the funding for my expenses to go to the national conference in November. With my expenses taken care of, our state association executive board would be left with more funding, which would give additional students from Alabama the opportunity to attend the national conferences. Much thought and evaluation went into making this decision, but ultimately, I decided to accept Jennifer's offer.

I was honored to be a member of the Advisory Committee, which consists of nine students from across the country. This committee makes recommendations to the NEA about the needs of the student program, which ultimately improves the program.

While, I was excited about the new opportunity, I knew I had to maintain my focus as President of the SAEA. Shortly thereafter, I was appointed to the Advisory Committee. To add more pressure, the SAEA's conference was scheduled to be located in Huntsville, Alabama where I attended college. The conference was hosted in downtown Huntsville at the Holiday Inn Select. I decided to take the lead in preparing for the conference by planning the "Outreach to Teach" project. Each year, the National Education Association Student Program members team up with retired educators to do a school makeover at a local school in the host city of the National Education Association's Representative Assembly.

I wanted to emulate those same charitable efforts in Huntsville. The school of choice was Ridgecrest Elementary.

In order for a school to receive support from the association they would have to be vetted by the student program organizer. Following the vetting process the state organizer would decide which school really fit what they were looking for. The procedure for contacting donors was very simple. To get the "Outreach to Teach" project process started, I wrote letters to local businesses requesting donations, discounts, and money to assist with the project. Many of the businesses provided donations and materials to assist with the project. For example, the store, School Craft, donated door prizes; Bennett's Nursery donated plants; Home Depot donated paint; Coca Cola donated free beverages; and Lowe's reduced their price for a pallet of wood chips. We were very blessed to have been given the materials for the project. In addition to getting the materials, we also had a record number of participants for the project. We had nearly 125 students participating throughout the state. After we finished the project the school looked amazing. As a result, our program started to flourish even more.

BRINGING PLANS TO FRUITION

It was the beginning of November 2005; the National Education Association Student Program (NEA-SP) hosted its fall Connection Conference in Boston, Massachusetts. This was one of the most enjoyable student conferences I have ever attended. The conference theme was "University of NEA-SP." I can remember it as if it was yesterday; there were students walking around wearing their perspective university's paraphernalia and the smell of excitement was in the air.

Although I was enthralled by all of the festivities held at the conference, I had to uphold my duties with the Advisory Committee in addition to completing my duties; I had secretly decided to make a run for Chairperson of the National Education Association Student Program. My closest friends within the program were the only confidants to whom I disclosed my interest to before announcing my candidacy.

In order for my plans to be brought to fruition, I organized a private meeting with the committed supporters that I've known for years.

After sharing my intentions with my friends, I sensed some doubt in the room. There were some that weren't sure that I could achieve this goal. Of course I understood that there were some who felt as though my chances weren't as promising, especially since this would be a historical feat. However, I continued to construct a plan of how I could win this position, as the first African American male. Following my presentation, I looked around the room at my supporters and I could clearly see that their reactions demonstrated hope for the future and a sense of change for the future of the organization. The question was then asked, "What can I do to help you win?" It was at this point that everyone in the room vowed to be with me, regardless of any doubt they may have had.

My faith and determination have always superseded my irrational judgments based on physical attributes, such as race. With that faith, I encouraged my supporters to believe and support my merits and work ethic. The group agreed to keep quiet until I officially declared my candidacy. While continuing to keep my decision to run for NEA Student Program Chairperson confidential, I was simultaneously trying to resolve a few issues within the Student Alabama Education Association. As I continued to focus on the conflict with state certification, I meanwhile visited a few campuses where I explained the requirements in great detail.

Despite any apprehensions regarding certification requirements, the SAEA was still able to accumulate a significant number of members. Many existing and new members were empowered by their chance to participate and exercise their voice at the Board meeting, intending to impede the new state certification requirements.

In order to speak at the board meeting, one must sign the log so that the Chair of the meeting would recognize them. Since each of us were passionate about our stance against the new state certification requirements, we each took a turn approaching the podium to state our position and personal confessions in regard to the Praxis II requirement. Although, the members of the state board listened to our stories and attempted to pacify our discontent, they ultimately decided to uphold their position on the Praxis II test requirement for certification. Following our testimonies we were able to change the mind of one Board member, but of course one vote wasn't enough to overturn the decision. This was a major disappointment but it made us feel empowered.

During my term as state President I was given several opportunities to travel out of the state. I traveled to the Ohio Student Education Association conference as well as the Georgia Association of Educators conference student program. I attended these conferences so that I might identify new ideas to bring back to the state of Alabama. My belief has always been that if I wanted to increase the interest and retain members, I must bring new effective ideas to the program.

DECLARING MY CANDIDACY

As my presidency of SAEA was nearing its conclusion, I began preparing to run for NEA-Student Program Chairperson. At the end of April 2006, two weeks before the May 1 deadline, I declared my candidacy for the position. Surprisingly, Jennifer Rogers, the Chair at the time, immediately contacted me by email and informed me that I was required to go through an interview process for the position. This initial email led to a chain of emails containing many contentious remarks made by Jennifer, which escalated my bewilderment and questions in regard to the correct process. Running for a national position such as this was unknown territory to me, but I felt I was being led in the wrong direction. Intuitively, I felt that Jennifer did not have my best intentions in mind.

I responded, "I was under the impression that this is an elected position which doesn't require an interview."

"This position is not what you think it is," she wrote back. "You really don't know what you're getting yourself into. Besides, I thought you wanted to go to law school. Please give me a call. I would like to talk to you about the position."

Quickly, I replied, "I do plan to go to law school. I talked about law school with my brother and he told me that law school would be there in the future, too. Also, could you please explain what you mean by, 'This position is not what I think it is'?"

After I responded to her initial email, Jennifer tried her best to pressure and intimidate me. Her behavior began to affect my position as an Advisory Committee member and I began to lose morale for my campaign. My run for Chairperson became very challenging as Jennifer began to hassle me and even discourage me not to run. I later learned that Jennifer's goal was to get her close friend elected as the Chairperson of the Student Program.

Although I was extremely irritated by her behavior, I continued to pursue my campaign. Unfortunately, I began my campaign with only $50, which I used to purchase a book of stamps, envelopes, a post office box, blank thank-you cards, labels, and typing paper. With my new supplies, I immediately began writing letters to individuals all over the state:

Fundraising Letter: May 15, 2006

Dear Sir or Madam:

I am writing you to invite you to consider making an individual contribution to my campaign as the National Educational Association-Student Program Chairperson (NEA-SP). NEA-SP is a national educational association group working to ensure proper preparation for students in teacher quality, political actions, and community outreach.

Why is an organization like National Education Association-Student Programs necessary? Here are some of the issues that the organization addresses:

- Preparing student leaders in education
- Teacher preparation
- Community involvement
- Political action for educational reform in public education

Experts in the political arena and educational community have called NEA-SP one of the most effective organizations working to train and educate future educators, leaders, and administrators. NEA-SP members are simply ordinary citizens like me who see themselves as champions of quality instruction to meet the needs of all educators.

I have worked with our elected officials, grass roots organizations, and educators on the local, state, and national level to support legislation, policies, and funding for educational training to foster the demands of student needs. My involvement with NEA-SP has shown me that my efforts make a difference. With our limited budget and staff, the organization has a powerful network of volunteers that have secured federal funding for successful, educational, and literacy programs in the United States and throughout the world.

The sense of hope and empowerment that I've had since joining NEA-SP has been very surprising. Since I have been more active as a citizen through the support of NEA-SP — calling and writing elected officials and organizational members — I see that our educational system really works. I have witnessed practical solutions to even seemingly overwhelming problems.

Because I have been a part of and have seen first hand the difference NEA-SP has been making in the lives of students and educators, I am asking for a donation for my election to the office of Chairperson. If paying by check, please make your donation payable to Anthony Daniels and forward it to the address below:

P. O. Box 61
Normal, AL 35762

This donation will go toward the duplication of print material, advertising, and travel, as well as other items needed in my campaign. I'll contact you personally in approximately one week to discuss your donation to my campaign. Regardless of whether you decide to fund this effort, I'm looking forward to soliciting your ideas and sharing my opinions on education with you.

Sincerely,

Anthony Daniels Jr.

After mailing letters to solicit donations, I went to the bank to open an account for my campaign. Then my next step was to find a treasurer for my campaign before the donations started coming in. My treasurer's name was Morgan. Her job was to collect all the donations, keep up with the receipts from all transactions of my campaign account, and write receipts to those that made donations. My strategy was to have one campaign manager in all six regions (Mid-Atlantic, Midwest, Southeast, Western, Pacific, and Northeast).

I had three opponents, two of whom were from the same region, and the other from a smaller region. I believed that if I wanted to have a chance at all, I would have to campaign in every state. I even campaigned in the state where my opponents were from. I did this to secure their vote in case of a run-off. I was determined to win this election regardless of what the cynics said. There were many state leaders that thought the Student Program Chairperson had already been decided. I was very fortunate that my campaign managers were in constant communication with the members in their regions.

The fundraising was going quite well for us. We started to see an influx of money coming in from within the state as well as from out of the state. Our totals had reached several thousand dollars after only two weeks of fundraising. With money coming in at such a fast pace, we felt very confident about our chances to win the election in the on-set.

NEFARIOUS TACTICS

The evening of my first fundraising event I received a vexing phone call from a restricted number. I allowed the phone to ring several times before answering it, "Hello, hello," in a low tone. The caller replied, "May I speak with Anthony Daniels please?" "This is he," I replied. "Anthony, this is Jennifer, Jessica, and Jackie (the NEA-Student Program Chairperson, Election Chair and Organizer). We are calling to inform you that you have been disqualified due to improper labeling on your campaign flier." Calmly, I responded by saying, "Okay, that's fine." Any campaign items that omit the name of the committee that paid for the items are considered a violation of the campaign rules. After hanging up the phone, I consulted with leadership within the organization. Fortunately, despite her tactics, I was reinstated back into the campaign.

The NEA Student Program election process is very similar to the nomination process for candidates seeking a nomination from their party. Each state's delegate allocations are based solely upon their states membership. For example, each state is allotted one delegate for the first 50 members, two delegates for the first 500 members, and for every 750 members after, they are entitled an additional delegate. Aspiring delegates are entitled to run within their state using the democratic process. Upon winning a statewide election, these individuals are then fully funded to attend the national convention, where they will then vote for Association leaders.

In the summer of 2006, the Student Leadership Conference took place in Orlando, Florida, which was approximately 45 miles north of where I once lived, Haines City, Florida. Days before the conference one of my campaign managers and I arrived to Orlando to gear up for the upcoming election. In the midst of our preparation rumors began to surface about who the next Chair would be. Unfortunately, the name mentioned was not "Anthony Daniels Jr." These rumors were disappointing, but I didn't allow them to discourage me.

After much anticipation, the opening night of the conference finally arrived. All candidates were to be nominated from the floor. Upon nomination, each candidate was expected to deliver a one-minute introductory speech. Each candidate for Student Program Chairperson had been nominated and had finished their introductory speeches. The Elections Chair gave one last call for other nominees by stating, "Are there any more candidates for the office of Chairperson of the NEA-Student Program?" My campaign manager, Jennie, then stood up and said, "I, Jennie, nominate Anthony Daniels Jr. for the office of Chairperson of the NEA-Student Program." Another student member approached the microphone and seconded it. The Elections Chair then asked me, "Do you accept this nomination?" I replied, "Yes, I accept."

I knew that if I wanted to win the election I had to give a very strong introductory speech. I had to give the audience reasons why I was the best candidate. I came prepared with the goal to change the minds of as many voters as possible. This was a very strenuous competition, mainly because I was facing the same candidates from the previous year.

Shortly after the Student Program Chairperson nominees were declared, the candidates for the Resolutions Committee and Board of Directors were called to the podium to give their speeches. Then candidates for Chairperson were called to the front to give their introductory speeches.

When writing my speech, I focused on inclusiveness as oppose to the positions I've held. Besides, it was evident that my opponents had more experience on the national than I did. So I stayed away from stating experience as a reason for supporting my candidacy. In contrast, my speech focused on the powerful definition of true leadership, diplomacy, and democracy. More importantly, I emphasized my encouragement for all student members to exercise their voice in order to make an impact not only within the National Education Association, but also within the nation as a whole. After I concluded my speech, the audience burst into applause and rose to their feet, giving me an emotional standing ovation. It was a proud moment.

Campaign Speech; June, 2006

Someone once described a leader as a person who cares more than others think is wise, risks more than others think is prudent, dreams more than others think is practical, and expects more than others think is possible (Claude T Bissell). As a leader we all know that faith without work is dead. Values are adopted through witnessing positive moral behavior. I know that not everything that is faced can be changed, but nothing can be changed until it is faced.

NEA has worked on six components: fix and fund, No Child Left Behind, closing the achievement gap, reaching out to minorities, cultivate grassroots support, improve teachers' salaries, and last but not least, building membership. In order to accomplish all we want to accomplish for our members, our schools, and our students, we need a growing and involved membership. Every association member should be prepared to answer questions from non-members and invite them to join. Every association leader is a membership organizer – from the new members to the local association officers to the state officer's to the national officers.

I remember the story told by Congressman James Clyburn of South Carolina. There was this boy who visited his grandfather every summer, and one particular summer he said to his grandfather, "I want to be just like you," and the grandfather replied by saying, "That's great son." So the little boy and his grandfather went to bed that night. Early the next morning the little boy's grandfather woke him up and said, "Let's go." So they went outside to feed the hogs, milk the cows, and get eggs from the chickens. Later that morning they came in for breakfast. The little boy looked at his grandfather and said, "Grandpa, are we done yet?" He looked at his grandson and said, "Son, those were just the chores. The real work is in the field."

So all the work that I've done leading up to now, from the local level, state level and the national level, were all chores and the real work would be on August 1, 2006 when I take the office of the NEA Student Program Chairperson.

MAKING ALLIANCES

Although the other candidates received applause, the crowd did not stand to their feet as they did for me. I was surprisingly overwhelmed about the crowd's reaction to my speech in comparison to my opponent's speeches, but I was confident I had their attention leaving the opening session. Afterwards, the Pennsylvania Student Education Association, the largest delegation attending the conference, approached me. They invited me to have dinner with them at a local restaurant. I accepted their invitation. However, I informed them of my need to go to my room.

When I got to the room I made calls to my campaign managers to inform them about my plans for the evening. I later assigned them to undecided states to target for potential votes. My campaign team really committed themselves to working all night to ensure my success. They organized supporters to wear our campaign T-shirts on a certain day, pass out materials and spread the word through text messaging. Our goal was to get every vote we could.

Before going to dinner with the Pennsylvania delegation, I called two of my opponents to invite them to dinner as well. On our way to dinner, I received many compliments for my speech. The members felt my passion and dedication for the organization and I could only hope to be given the opportunity to prove my dedication if elected.

Throughout dinner we spent time introducing ourselves to each other. We shared our experiences in college and stories about our families. I was thoroughly enjoying my company. It was the first time during the conference that I had allowed my personality to show as opposed to constantly organizing and discussing my campaign. I have always believed that the best strategy to campaigning is by building relationships with your constituents.

Unaware of the hours that had past, it wasn't until the closing hours that we decided to call it a night. As we were leaving the restaurant, a student leader from the Pennsylvania delegation stated, "Anthony, you have our vote and I think I speak for the entire group when I say this; you are the best candidate we've heard tonight. We believe you will represent us well." "I promise I will not let you down. I will do my best to turn this program around and take us in the right direction," I replied.

INSIDE THE CAMPAIGN

The following morning was the Outreach to Teach project, whereby student members attending the conference dedicate time to cleaning, decorating, and revitalizing a public school in need. The Outreach to Teach project is an all day event that requires a lot of physical work and commitment. Eccelston Elementary School, in Orlando, Florida was the fortunate school chosen for the project. Student members participated in painting walls, murals, and reviving the landscaping.

Following the Outreach to Teach project was the awards banquet, scheduled for later that evening. The awards banquet is a traditionally formal and ceremonious event. The banquet setting appeared to be taken directly out of an enchanted fairy tale picture book. It was a very attractive event full of class and sophistication. All of the student members were very polished and well dressed in their most elegant and dashing attire. Although it was an attractive event with lavish amenities in a luxurious setting with the finest cuisine and service, ultimately, it was a professional business event, whereby each state was anticipating receiving awards for their great efforts within the organization.

Each student leader and active member was looking forward to being recognized for his or her outstanding undertakings. As the night proceeded, I started to take notice of the unusual amount of awards one particular state was winning. It seemed as though this state had a monopoly on the awards banquet. I began to have an uncanny feeling that the organizers of the awards banquet had failed to observe traditional standards or show due honesty. It was my intuition that the awards banquet had been set-up with a pre-arranged outcome. Many student leaders across the nation were anticipating the "Outstanding State Student Leader" award, but it went to the student leader of this particular state nonetheless. Coincidentally, the student leader from this state was a candidate for the NEA-SP and was also close friends with Jennifer, the current Chairperson. This particular state had received an abundant amount of recognition at the awards assembly and I still strongly believe that this was Jennifer's attempt to persuade voters to support this state's state leader in the national race. I was convinced Jennifer was a conspirator in this ploy. She had been ardently promoting this candidate while fervidly attempting to disqualify me. Many participants expressed their frustration of the results. After all, it was hard to believe that one state was the best in every category.

Immediately following the awards banquet, I called a meeting with my campaign managers to discuss a strategy for my run. We spent a lot of time putting together our floor strategy for distributing campaign materials to student members. One piece of campaign propaganda was intended to reach elementary education majors. This publicity included a pamphlet, which displayed a "KWL" chart. The "KWL" chart stands for, "What you Know," "What you Want to Know," and "What you Learned." My version of the chart included the "K", which stood for, "What you Know about Anthony," "W" represented, "What you Want to know about Anthony," and the "L" denoted, "What you Learned about Anthony." A color portrait of me assisting a student during my internship was presented on the front of the pamphlet. This unique brochure received a lot of attention. Other influential materials included bottle openers, t-shirts, rulers, and car magnets.

The morning of the candidate's speeches, the energy was high and the supporters were anxiously waiting to hear each candidate's platform and plan for change. Prior to the speeches, my campaign workers carefully distributed the campaign materials out on the tables and on the chairs where the delegates and student members would be seated. Out of 250 student members present during the speeches, at least 100 members wore my campaign t-shirts throughout the day. Twenty-five out of those 100 were delegates elected to vote. Even many students who weren't wearing a t-shirt were requesting to have one. Many other students wanted a shirt to wear but we didn't have anymore. Our floor strategy was a successful pursuit for publicizing my campaign.

Unexpectedly, prior to the candidate speeches, the current Election's Chair addressed the audience to make an emergency announcement of candidates who were disqualified and why. My name was called among the candidates who were announced. This message was completely false in regard to my campaign because I had previously been dishonorably and unjustifiably disqualified, which had already been resolved in June. It was now July and the Election's Chair is misinformed and misspeaking with regard to my campaign on the day of the election. Again, I believe this was another devious tactic used by the Elections Chair and Student-Program Chairperson to undermine the integrity of my campaign and the campaign of others. As a result of the announcement, many state delegates were confused about who they could vote for since their candidates were eliminated from the race. These abrupt announcements led to much confusion, chaos, and uncertainty within the entire conference. This announcement negatively affected my campaign because the Election's Chair failed to mention or was uninformed that I had been reinstated two weeks prior to the conference after my attorney tended to the previous disqualification. This strange sequence of events during the election had become a mental strain. I was being challenged by situations that I had never experienced before, but I remained determined to persevere through these challenges.

I continued to participate in the race regardless of the inaccurate announcement in regard to my campaign. Therefore, as the candidate speeches began, I sat in the back of the room until they asked the candidates for Chairperson to leave the room and wait for their name to be called to speak. I was determined to give the best speech I could possibly give. When my name was called, I went into the room and gave my speech.

Again, the student members were very receptive to my words of encouragement and passion for the organization and I was shown their appreciation through another warm and energetic standing ovation.

I then responded to the questions asked by the Elections Chair submitted by other conference attendees. Even though I gave my speech and answered questions about my intentions with the organization, the delegates were still unsure if their votes would be counted if they cast their ballots for me.

The situation was rectified during lunch. The auditorium was filled with college students when the polls were open. A young woman stood up looking irritated and begrudgingly began to ask, "Are the candidates disqualified? Are they still disqualified? Can we vote for them? Do we have to select from the remaining candidates?" Thankfully, the rapid execution of these questions forced the Elections Chair to explain and correct her false statements made prior to lunch. She repeated her earlier announcement, but followed up with, "You guys can vote for the candidates that were disqualified." With only thirty minutes to vote, the students lined up with a sense of urgency. My supporters were at the polls to do some last minute campaigning.

Immediately after the polls closed, the Elections Committee began to count the ballots. As I anticipated the results, I approached two of my opponents and told them, "No matter what the results are, we must vow to remain friends regardless of what happens." Shortly after, the Elections Chair approached the stage. The room went completely silent. She first announced the winners for the Resolutions Committee and Board of Directors positions. Gleeful sounds of victory and excitement filled the room as those names were announced. The room was filled with the sense of bittersweet exuberance and suspense as the student members awaited the decision of the position for Student Program Chairperson. The Elections Chair then read the number of votes cast for Chairperson and said, "With over fifty-percent of the votes, the winner of the position of NEA Student Program Chairperson is Anthony Daniels."

When the results were called I paused in disbelief. The feeling was so surreal. I stood up in front of my seat, raised my head to the ceiling, and jovially exclaimed, "Thank you Lord! Thank you Lord!" The entire room jumped in the air with jubilation. The response from the crowd was a sight comparable to the crowd at the end of a championship game. Even my opponents walked up to me, hugged me, and whispered, "Congratulations" in my ear. The entire room paraded around me. I received hug after hug from folks all around the room. This was the happiest day of my life! I had been dreaming about being there for so long but now it was finally real!

This was definitely an exciting time in my life. I was taking pictures with different people and as I walked around the room, I thanked all of my campaign managers and supporters. I even thanked those who didn't support me. I told them that we were going to work together to take the program light years ahead of its time. After taking more pictures with delegates, I was interviewed by someone from NEA-Public Relations. The reporter asked about my plans for the office. I replied, "I would like to make college affordable for Americans and I would like to see stipends for student teachers. I would also like to see teacher pay increase."

After doing the interview with the reporter, I then went to my room to collect my thoughts. I was overwhelmed with excitement and joy. I was so grateful. I was previously faced with so much adversity and I was able to overcome it. My faith and spirit were beat down, but they were never broken down. After celebrating with myself, I got down on my knees to thank God for allowing me this opportunity to represent 62,000 students enrolled in over 1,100 colleges and universities nationwide. I told God that I would do everything in my power to move this program to another level.

While in my room, I received a number of phone calls from individuals from all around the country congratulating me on winning the election. Later that evening, I went to a retirement reception where I was introduced to NEA retired members. When I returned to the hotel, I was asked to come to the pool to hang out. When I arrived to the pool, I was greeted by NEA student members. They rallied together to give me a festive celebration for the victory I had achieved. It was a pool party with pizza, decorations and music. I was very happy that they acknowledged me. I was so elated by this positive recognition. Their acceptance of me showed that together, we could take this program to heights never before reached.

TAKING THE REIGN

After the election, I received a phone call from Reg Weaver, the President of the National Education Association. He asked me if I would be interested in attending a research program for the National Equity Center. I was honored by his invitation and flattered that he instantly thought of me. I went to UCLA to conduct research for the National Equity Center. This was a unique experience for me because I worked beside some highly intelligent students from various diverse backgrounds from across the country. The program required a lot research and reading. Two weeks into the program, I received a phone call and email from a representative with the National Education Association, directing me to prepare my belongings for the move to Washington, D.C., which is where I was assigned to reside during my new two-year tenure as the Chairperson for the NEA Student Program.

Moving to D.C. required that I immediately leave California, return to Alabama, pack, and withdraw from college. I was taking risks and making sacrifices but I believed it to be well worth it. Regretfully, I had to cut my time at UCLA short to begin moving in order to be in D.C. by July 27, 2006.

Even though I was saddened about leaving the state of California, simultaneously, I was excited to embark on a new journey in a location, which I had previously dreamed of residing. When I was a freshman in college, I attended a NASA Pre-service Teachers Conference in Alexandria, Virginia, whereby I participated in several professional development workshops which encouraged teachers and prospective teachers to integrate more science and math into the classroom through cross-curriculum activities. While visiting Alexandria, I fell in love with the 18th and 19th century architecture, historical ambience and modern amenities, professional demeanor of its citizens, and its proximity to the nation's capital. All that the city had to offer captivated me; I knew instantly that I wanted to eventually live there one day. During that trip I had begun to think of avenues that would lead me to this location in my future. I wanted to be apart of Alexandria and the Metropolitan area so much that I had even dreamed of it in my sleep. My dreams had come true. I won the election for Chairperson of the National Education Association and was scheduled to live in Alexandria, Virginia and work in the National Education Association Headquarters in the heart of our nation's capital.

I was so excited to be living in Alexandria, Virginia and working in Washington, D.C. I felt very blessed to be given this opportunity. This area was so drastically different from Alabama and definitely a culture shock.

The Metropolitan area is a large population center consisting of a very large and densely populated industrial and commercial city with several closely adjoining neighboring central cities. Just like most visitors in the nation's capital, I was impressed by its grandeur. As I became more acquainted with the area, I discovered the exciting city beyond the monuments and museums. Washington D.C. is rich in culture, recreational opportunities, and history. This was a huge culture shock to me as well. Almost three quarters of the population within the city are employed in white-collar jobs, something that I wasn't accustomed to seeing growing up in Alabama. Half of the working population is between the ages of 25-49, the youngest working population in the country. It was refreshing to see that the city offered something for everyone. It catered to an array of cultures, religions, lifestyles, and interests. I felt very privileged to be in the heart of it all.

While enjoying all the wonders Washington, D.C. and the Metropolitan area had to offer, I began to notice the dense proportion of homelessness within the city. I had never seen homelessness like that before in Alabama. Those individuals had nothing. I noticed individuals lingering around the monuments and public facilities sleeping or begging for change. Many of these individuals cannot afford or are otherwise unable to maintain, regular, safe, and adequate shelter.

As I noticed their inhabitance within the city, I started to realize that there are many social problems these people face such as violent crimes, reduced access to health care, discrimination, unemployment, and difficulties obtaining access to transportation or technology. I realized that this issue exists all over the nation, and one way I decided I could help with this issue was to continue to promote and foster my belief in helping our youth obtain a meaningful education to achieve the American dream.

My first day in the office was August 1, 2006. I began the day by becoming acclimated to my office. I became acquainted with using the telephone system, using the computer, and operating the elevator. Fortunately, there were individuals assigned to help me learn these tasks quickly. After learning the phone system, I decided to call my family and inform them of my arrival. Members of my family expressed concern for my well-being and safety. After all, Washington D.C. is well-known as the murder capital of the United States. I comforted them by describing my safe neighborhood in Alexandria, Virginia and then explained the extensive security at the NEA building. I could confidently assure them that I was far from dangerous crime stricken neighborhoods. Shortly after chatting with my family, I called the NEA-SP Organizational specialist, who is an advisor to the Student Program Chairperson, and asked her if she would make appointments for me to meet with the following departments: Public Relations, Teacher Quality, and Governance and Policy, since meetings were already arranged for me to meet with the NEA officers.

My first meeting was with the NEA President, Reg Weaver. I asked him if he would mentor me. He replied by saying, "Certainly." He graciously assured me that he would help me. His last words were, "I'm available for you anytime you need my assistance." My second meeting was with Dennis Van Roekel, the Vice President of the NEA. He too promised to be there for me. "However, there's one request Anthony," he said. "You will need to maintain the student program orientation booklet for your successor." My third meeting was with the NEA's Secretary Treasurer, Lily Eskelsen. She generously vowed to provide me with the assistance needed to be successful. After meeting with the NEA Executive officers I began to feel very confident in the progression of the organization.

My first year in office, I spent at least 12 to 13 hours in the office each day except for when I was on travel. My goal was to understand the organizational structure, hierarchy, and bureaucratic processes in order to fulfill my vision for the Student Program. I began taking notes and writing outlines to implement my strategy on paper in order to better execute it. I was interested in resolving the political issues relating to public education as well as access to affordable college. The issues of making college affordable and increasing teacher salaries had become a barrier, which severely reduced the amount of students enrolling in the field of education as a profession. These disparaging ramifications led to the decline of highly qualified teachers in the classroom. Therefore, I decided to take on the issue of making college affordable.

I initiated my plan by meeting with different department directors in order to build interdepartmental partnerships. Each department head pledged to work closely with the Student Program in accomplishing its goals and objectives.

"Focusing on the weaknesses and building on the strengths," has always been a leadership strategy of mine. The specific weaknesses were teacher quality, community outreach, and political action. But before we could initiate tackling these challenges, the Student Program had to focus on membership, communication, and logistical complications.

One of my first major tasks as Chairperson was to make committee recommendation to Reg Weaver, the NEA President. I wrote letters of recommendation for individuals, which included my reason for recommendation, a brief biography about the person, a description of their involvement within the organization, and their original letter of recommendation to me. I wrote recommendations for committees such as the Advisory Committee, the Employee Advocacy Committee, the Membership committee, and the Human and Civil Rights committee. While all of the committee's were important, I chaired the Advisory

Committee of Student Members. The Advisory Committee makes recommendations to the NEA Board of Directors, dealing with changes affecting the Student Program, and monitors the program's services and delivery system. Therefore, the selection process was very strategic in order to recommend the most efficient leaders. I told many applicants, "If you're not ready to work, and work hard, you might want to recall your applications." After considerable assessment and deliberation, the Advisory Committee appointees were adopted because of my recommendation without any objections from the NEA Board of Directors. I congratulated the committee and told them, "It is evident that your commitment to this association is unwavering."

The Advisory Committee consisted of ten members including myself. These diverse student members were from different regions of the country and were able to offer various perspectives and talents to the committee. As the Chairperson presiding over the committee, I was responsible for coordinating the activities of the Advisory Committee emphasizing NEA visibility on campuses and organizing the future of the NEA active members. They were given specific charges to focus on. Charges are areas that the NEA Student Chairperson had identified as weaknesses within the organization. It was imperative that these charges were corrected in order to strengthen and maintain order within the NEA Student Program. Thankfully, prior to being the Student Program Chairperson, I was a member of the Advisory Committee under the leadership of Jennifer Rogers'. I learned about the needs of the organization by observing the organization's weaknesses. Furthermore, I was able to utilize my experience and discretion to create charges prior to selecting the proper committee members.

One imperative charge was recruiting and retaining members into the Student Program while placing specific emphasis on ethnic minorities. An additional charge was recruiting and retaining freshmen and sophomore members. There had been a huge deficiency within these areas for years and it was my belief that increasing freshmen and sophomores within local chapters would sustain our organization and inherently strengthen the Student Program. Moreover, I believed that a significant minority presence within the Student Program would foster, promote, and enhance ethnic minority involvement in local, state, regional, and national association activism and leadership. Once the charges were established, the responsibilities were allocated proportionately. Throughout my term we continuously strived to promote community partnerships, foster leadership, promote membership among diverse populations, and provide networking opportunities for our members. In addition, politically, we focused on college affordability to ultimately support and increase our aspiring educators and potential members.

We believed the issue of college affordability directly impacts millions of college students around the country. The majority of us were leaving school with an exponential amount of debt due to college loans. I left school with $58,000 in student loan debt. There are too many students around the country affected by this issue, especially those majoring in education. While the cost of college and student loan interest rates have been rising, the amount awarded for the Pell Grant remained at only $4,310, which causes a financial barrier to individuals pursuing public service careers such as teaching, nursing, law enforcement, and social work. The Advisory Committee collectively believed in addressing the college affordability crisis because we realized our country would experience tremendous shortages in public service.

The Department of Education held hearings throughout the nation in order to address the issue of making college affordable. However, during the final hearing I was invited to testify on behalf of the National Education Association. After being invited to testify at the hearing, I felt a bit uneasy about the amount of people present and what I would say. I knew I had a lot to say about the issue but didn't know exactly how I wanted say it. It was three days before the testimony that I finally put my words on paper. After writing the testimony, I then asked a friend and co-worker to review my remarks for accuracy and flow. He reviewed my testimony and made some adjustments to it.

The day before the testimony I asked another friend of mine about the conditions of a testimony. He explained to me the testimonies he witnessed a few years back. He went on to assure me that I had nothing to worry about. He said, "It will go by really fast. However, one piece of advice that I will give you is to make sure you stick to the script." I took his advice and continued to practice reading my testimony.

I arrived to the room in which I was summoned to testify. I sat down on a bench beside several other students from local universities around D.C. because they were there to testify as well. After taking my seat I looked around the room to see if it was as I had envisioned. It wasn't like I envisioned; I thought there would be chairs, desks and microphones aligned for the speakers to give their testimonies. Instead, the room had rows of chairs, standing microphone in the isles, all overseen by a panel of officials listening to the testimonies. As I waited in my seat, I heard my name called over the speaker, "Anthony Daniels, the next testimony will be given by Anthony Daniels." I stood up, walked to the podium and began my testimony.........

Testimony: Department of Education

November 8, 2006

Dear Ms. Macias,

Thank you for convening these hearings about how to make college affordable. I am both professionally and personally concerned about the issue of fair and manageable student loan repayment rules. Professionally, I currently serve as the Chairperson of the National Education Association's Student Program, where I represent over 60,000 students on over 1,100 college and university campuses preparing for careers in education. The rising levels of student debt threaten their ability to pursue successful careers in education without being committed to lengthy student loans plagued by rising interest rates.

Personally, we are all concerned about the large levels of student loan debt. As a recent graduate with an outstanding level of student loan debt I am affected personally by the cost and concerns of repayment plans. I received my Bachelors' degree in Elementary Education in spring 2005 from Alabama A&M University in Normal, Alabama, and am currently pursuing a Masters' degree in Special Education at the same institution. After completing my Bachelors' degree in four years, I found myself over thirty thousands dollars in loan repayment debt. At that point I wondered how I could possibly survive on a first year teacher salary of $28,000 in the state of Alabama. I even asked myself, "Was college the best way to go or should I have looked for a regular job?" Working a regular job did not seem so bad after all. At least I would be making a better living without the stress of loan repayments. But that decision had been made. I had to look at the situation I was in after graduation. I looked at my $30,000 of debt, extremely low teacher salaries, and decided that my only option was to further my education so I would be able to get more money. I saw this as my best option because having just finished my student teaching two weeks earlier; I could not see how I could possibly afford to travel to another state for an interview, or pay relocation fees should I actually be offered a job.

The teaching profession is a calling from within. I went into teaching because it is the most rewarding profession in the world. There is nothing more exciting than helping students discover things that fascinate them, and nothing is more rewarding than seeing a child grasp an idea and develop an idea of his or her own. But how can I purchase a house or a car when I am already over $30,000 in debt? This is a major concern for all of my colleagues.

More than eight million post-secondary students receive financial aid, with 70 percent of this support coming from the federal government. In the next decade, undergraduate enrollment in colleges and universities will increase by 14 percent, with 80 percent of these new students coming from minority backgrounds, and one in five living in poverty. Federal aid is already insufficient to allow all who want to pursue higher education to do so. Recent studies have indicated the typical student borrower leaves school almost $20,000 in debt, and that many young Americans face such significant college debt that they defer homeownership and starting a family. Fewer and fewer are able to take on careers in teaching, social work, or other public interest fields.

I am attaching a table taken from the State PIRGs' Higher Education Project report *Paying Back, Not Giving Back: Student Debt's Negative Impact on Public Service Career Opportunities.* The table shows the percentage of college graduates who would have unmanageable debt if they took a teaching job in each state. Nationally, nearly a quarter of graduates from public 4-year institutions will have unmanageable debt on a starting teacher's salary, and the figure rises to almost 40% of the graduates from private 4-year institutions. Higher education remains a critical investment for young people to make in themselves; for families to make in the success of their children; and for the nation to make in its future. Current projections are that financial barriers will prevent 4.4 million high school graduates from attending a 4-year public college over the next decade and will prevent another 2 million high school graduates from attending any college at all. I recognize that this is a complicated problem and that much of this responsibility lies within the purview of the President, Congress, and the states. To date, the federal government has not been doing its part to help make college affordable. Last February, Congress passed a measure that removed almost $12 billion from federal student aid programs and in his FY 2007 budget, the President proposed $1.2 billion in additional cuts to higher education programs. It is putting it mildly to say that we have been very disappointed with these actions by both the White House and Congress. The latest cuts have further exacerbated the affordability of a college education, leaving many lower-income students unable to complete their education.

As we look for solutions to this problem, we applaud the recommendations in the recent report of the Secretary's Commission on the Future of Higher Education to highlight access and affordability, especially the recommendation to increase the nation's commitment to need-based aid. However, as NEA President Reg Weaver says, "To give the proposal teeth we need a commitment from lawmakers to provide adequate funding." In order to meet broader higher education goals, NEA also calls for improving student preparation and providing more high schools with programs on adolescent literacy and dropout prevention, as well as counseling, smaller learning communities and an expansion of AP courses. Kathy Sproles, President of the National Council for Higher Education, added, "The benefits of higher education are much more than bigger paychecks for the graduate or a stronger economy. Higher education is key to promoting an informed citizenry and protecting our democratic society." NEA hopes to continue working with the Department in this area, and looks forward to next spring's summit on higher education announced in Secretary Spelling's speech last September.

The Department can do its part on this issue by taking some concrete steps, but it cannot do it alone. NEA will be working to increase grant aid, and other student aid programs in order to increase college affordability. As Chair of the NEA Student Program, I pledge to contribute to that effort. Cutting interest rates in half on student and parent college loans, as well as increasing grant aid, are important steps toward reversing the recent cuts to higher education assistance.

One step the Department can take is to make changes in loan repayment terms that would provide more fair and manageable circumstances for college graduates once they begin to repay their loans. This would be a welcome result from this round of negotiated rulemaking. I thank you for your time, and I look forward to the continuing development of this process.

CEASING OPPORTUNITY

My first conference as Chairperson was on November 10-12, 2006 in Denver, Colorado at the Hyatt Regency Hotel. At this conference I informed student members about my testimony in front of officials from the Department of Education. After informing them of what lay ahead, I went on to motivate them of how with their help we were going to have the most exciting year of student program history. My ultimate intentions were to stimulate the audience by introducing the goals of the College Affordability Campaign and to promote active involvement in our program.

Also during the conference I asked students members to text the word "Student" to 35328 in order for them to receive text message updates about the campaign. I also promised to only send them no more than two messages per month unless it was an emergency. I continued to talk about the issue of making college affordable, but more so about them participating in the efforts to bring it to fruition. I went on to assure them that together we can get Congress to cut interest rates on student loans, increase the Pell grant for low income and middle income students and provide loan forgiveness for public service employees. I promised that those things would happen before I left office. My words of encouragement created enthusiasm among the student members as they left the conference. Student members departed from the conference pumped up and ready to fight with one mission in mind, to make college affordable.

The week of November 16, 2006 was "American Education Week." During this week, I returned to my old high school, Bullock County High School. I was invited to speak during American Education Week. My speech was written to motivate students to stay in school and realize their potentials to live the American dream. In my speech, I shared words of encouragement to the students by expressing to them that all things were possible and that they could achieve any goals that they set for themselves. I reminded them, however, that they must apply themselves in order to accomplish it.

Following my speech I went into the teachers' lounge where my tenth grade teacher Ms. Ivy had prepared a scrumptious meal. While in the lab, I was approached by several students that complimented me on my speech. I can remember one young man in particular saying, "Mr. Daniels how do I get to where you are? I know your message was about education and encouragement, but how does a young man with a C average, a mother that only has a sixth grade education, and a family that's waiting on me to finish high school so that I can work in the cotton mill in order to bring more money into the household get to where you are? Plus, if I start at 18, I could be a supervisor." I paused for a brief second and looked around the room and said, "Young man, don't let anyone tell you that you have to settle for just a high school diploma because you only have a C average. I only made a 14 on the ACT with a B average and look where I am today. Please don't be mistaken; I had folks telling me similar stories, but I found out through others that I had the ability to be somebody great. My advice to you is to take the ACT, study harder and apply to colleges until you get accepted. Success is failure turned inside out. We have all struggled at some point in time, but we got back up and kept on going. And this is what you will need to do throughout your entire life my brother."

The following Saturday, I spoke at the Illinois Education Association-Student Program State Conference in Edwardsville, Illinois. It was my first speech for the NEA-Student Program following the Connections Conference. While speaking, I encouraged the students to be a part of the fight to make college more affordable. I told them that together we could move mountains and encouraged them to take action by going to the Student Program website to lobby congress online. I closed my speech by asking them to take out their cell phones and text the word "Student" to 35328 and receive updates. This would be the practice everywhere I went.

I continued to spread the message of making college more affordable, but I felt I wasn't making enough noise. So I started attending weekly meetings with the NEA Government Relations department to see if the college affordability issue was making any traction on Capitol Hill. I learned that Congress was aware of the issue of college affordability, but resolving the issue wasn't a top priority. This inspired me to begin making visits to Capitol Hill to lobby members of Congress and their staff. After speaking with the staffers of several members of Congress, I then scheduled a sit down meeting with one of Alabama's leading Congressman, Artur Davis. After meeting with Congressman Davis I felt assured that this was a good issue to organize around. So, I took a mental note of our conversation and knew that I had to act fast. However, before our meeting ended I asked Congressman Davis if he would be willing to do an interview with me around the college affordability issue. "I would love to," he replied. My interview with Congressman Davis was scheduled that January. I was pleased to make a connection with Congressman Artur Davis, who had become an advocate to make college affordable. I was pleased to be publicizing this issue on Capitol Hill and expanding awareness of the need to make college more affordable.

Expanding awareness of the College Affordability Campaign had been a major project for the Advisory Committee of Student Members during my term in office. Soon after the text messaging campaign was implemented to spread information about college affordability, the Advisory Committee implemented another technological strategy through the use of Facebook. Facebook is an interactive social networking website designed to allow people to communicate and send information instantly to large quantities of people. The Facebook group entitled, "College Affordability Concerns Me," was created to publicize the issue of college affordability on a broader range. The Facebook group along with the text messaging campaign helped to educate and influence college students during the 2006 elections. Group members were encouraged to become more politically active by supporting their local political candidates. The Advisory Committee sent messages to students who subscribed to the 'Facebook' group and text campaign. They were advised who to vote for locally and given descriptions of the candidates' educational platforms.

On January 3, 2007, I conducted an interview with Congressman Artur Davis in the NEA television studio. I asked him a series of questions in regard to his stance on making college affordable. Congressman Davis explained that every student deserves to live in a country where they have an opportunity to achieve the American dream. In addition, he assured me that the 110th United States Congress would address the issue. A few days after my meeting with Congressman Davis I sent a memo out to student members updating them about the progress of the campaign.

Days after the memo was sent, I scheduled a meeting with the manager of the Student Program, Malcolm Staples. I expressed my new ideas for getting student members actively involved in the College Affordability Campaign. I usually turned to Malcolm when I needed honest advice. I went to him with the idea of allowing student members to become a part of a lobbying effort and press conference. After giving my synopsis about the importance of the involvement of student members in the process, Malcolm was convinced that this would be a great opportunity for student members to participate in political action.

He was impressed with my ideas and supported me in my endeavors.

Now there were some that thought it was impossible to get students involved in the political process and felt that I would be wasting my term trying to do so. However, I've always been under the assumption that nothing is impossible. Often times individuals are discouraged by critics and those that believe that things should be done the same way every year.

One day I was in my office making phone calls soliciting volunteers and one of my co-workers dropped by to talk. She walked in the office and said, "Anthony, students aren't really interested in politics; they only care about things that affect them right now. Besides, we've tried to get them involved before." "With all do respect sister, I'm a student and I don't want to be told what to do and how to do it. How would you feel if someone was always telling you what to do and how to do it? Would you feel empowered?" I replied. "No." she answered. "Well, this is the same way my colleagues feel. They would like to be involved but no one really asks for their support. It's not that we're apathetic; it's just that we haven't been given many opportunities to participate."

After our conversation, I continued to work diligently on the campaign with fresh ideas and new technologies. Malcolm kept his vow to support me in my efforts. One way he helped was by assigning three brilliant people to work on the College Affordability Campaign. He commissioned Kimberly, Don, and Mark, to work directly with the issue of college affordability. I was grateful for Malcolm's reliability and support. He had become a major asset in this campaign.

On the morning of January 11, 2007, there were six student members flown in to participate in the College Affordability Campaign. Upon their arrival to the NEA building, they were debriefed on how to lobby Congress. We created and studied a target list of congressmen who were rumored to vote against any bill that would cut lender subsidies.

We traveled to Capitol Hill and lobbied our targeted list of Congressional offices from 8:30 a.m. until 12:20 p.m. going from office to office, dropping off letters urging members to support a bill that would increase the Pell Grant and cut student loan interest rates in half. After our lobbying expedition, we had a chance to mingle with several key members of Congress. I was able to express my appreciation of their efforts to make college more affordable.

Following our visit on Capitol Hill, I had a chance to speak at a press conference which consisted of five student representatives and three members of Congress. The five student representatives included, Jen Pae (United States Student Association), Andrew Bossier (University of Southern Maine Student Body President), Jay Bhatt (President of American Medical Student Association), Paul Perry (Advisory Board member for Campus Progress), and myself, representing the National Education Association Student Program. The members of the Senate and House were Senator Ted Kennedy (MA), Congressman George Miller (CA), and Congressman Joe Courtney (CT).

When the press conference began, cameras were flashing, tape recorders and video cameras were rolling, and reporters were writing. I thought I would be nervous about speaking behind members of Congress, but I wasn't. I had concerns about college affordability like many students across the nation and this was the perfect opportunity for me to express it. The speaking line-up was structured to allow Congressmen and students to speak in intervals. When it came time for me to speak, I began by asking my fellow student leaders to join me at the podium. I introduced each of them individually by name, state, and school. I properly introduced myself to the audience and began to plea my case for college affordability as follows:

Press Conference Remarks; January 11, 2007

My name is Anthony Daniels, and I am currently pursuing a Masters' degree in Special Education at Alabama A & M where I received my Bachelors' degree in Elementary Education in 2005.

I am also the Chairperson of the National Education Association Student Program. Our program represents more than sixty thousand students who are studying at colleges and universities to become teachers. Six leaders from the program are here with us today, and I'd like to acknowledge them at this point:

> Ngoc Le from University of California, Los Angeles
> Todd Roberts from Emporia State University in Kansas,
> Amelia Sims from Alabama State University,
> Jennie Levy from Florida State University, and
> Willie Allen from Georgia Southwestern State University
> Kristi Uzzo from Southern Illinois University, Edwardsville

Like most of these students, I chose a career in teaching because it is the most rewarding profession in the world. There is nothing more exciting than helping children learn things that ignite their imagination and spark their curiosity. Unfortunately, the joy that comes from teaching doesn't pay the bills.

The average starting salary for teachers in my home state of Alabama is twenty-eight thousand dollars. And when I graduated with my four-year teaching degree from Alabama A&M University, I owed thirty thousand dollars in student loans. I wasn't an exception. The typical student who borrows to pay for a college education graduates with a debt of almost twenty thousand dollars.

That debt is a burden for most students – but for those of us who want to teach, it's more than a burden – it is a barrier.

It's hard enough to live on a starting teacher's salary – and it becomes almost impossible when we are saddled by debt from student loans. Nearly one-fourth of the new teachers who graduate from public universities will owe more in student loans than they can repay on a starting teacher's salary. For those who attend private universities, four out of every ten will have unmanageable debt.

The result is that we lose thousands of good teachers every year – people who want to teach, but can't afford to repay their student loans on a teacher's pay. Studies show that one-third of all new teachers leave the profession within the first five years. And the main reason cited by those who quit teaching is the difficulty of making ends meet.

This means fewer experienced teachers in the classroom. And that means our children are the ones who ultimately pay the price. Every year we hear about the shortage of good teachers. School systems across the country are trying many innovative ways to attract new people to the profession.

But one researcher has compared those efforts to pouring water into a bucket that has a hole in the bottom.

As long as teachers can't afford to pay their bills and their debts, the bucket will never get full. And our children won't get the experienced teachers they deserve.

Let's help our teachers and our children by making college affordable.

Let's lighten the burden of student loans, and remove the barrier to those who want to teach our children.

The very next day, the house introduced a bill that would cut interest rates on student loans, increase the Pell Grant, and provide "Teach Grants" for students going into the teaching profession. I used emails and Facebook to move students into action. I also had the text messaging company send out messages advising student members to urge their state representatives to support the College Affordability Bill, also known as House of Representatives Bill 5, through cyber lobbying, phone calls, or in writing. For the first time in NEA Student Program history, student members were making groundbreaking efforts in unparalleled exertions to influence political agendas for the sake of higher education. The bill passed the House!

However, our work was not yet complete. The bill needed to go through the entire bill passage process. In order for it to pass both the House and the Senate and be signed by the President, we needed to continue to publicize the cause, and through the use of technology we could do so both expeditiously and efficiently. Therefore, I requested a meeting with Don in order to impose new strategies for organizing and transmitting information about the bill to students through technology. He proposed that we continue to work diligently with various well-known interactive websites such as Facebook, Moveon. org, and other well-known bloggers. I also suggested that we develop a brand, logo, and slogan for the campaign and post them on materials such as t-shirts, bracelets, pamphlets, and even our own website. The goal was to create national exposure in our efforts to making college more affordable and accessible.

In the meantime, the Advisory Committee continued to keep students informed of the issues through newsletters and by word of mouth. I traveled throughout the country to different conferences discussing college affordability and promoted activism among student members. I challenged students across the nation to be a part of the solution to correct this problem by getting involved. I visited Columbus, Ohio, Orlando, Florida and Perdido Beach, Alabama where I promoted and advocated the college affordability campaign. I traveled to the Georgia Association of Educators Student Program in Athens, GA; the Mississippi Association of Educators where I visited Alcorn State University, Jackson State University, University of Mississippi, and the University Mississippi De Soto campus. Following this, I went to the Kansas National Education Association Student Program State Conference in Emporia, Kansas; San Jacinto College in Laporte, Texas; the Student Maine Education Association State Conference in Portland Standish, Maine; the Youth Education Society in Detroit, Michigan, and Mount San Antonio College in Rowland Heights, California; all to spread the word of making college more affordable.

Letter to the Senate; March 15, 2007

Dear Senator:

We are state leaders from the National Education Association Student Program (NEASP) who are in Washington this week to discuss issues pertaining to the future of the Higher Education Act (HEA.) NEASP is a nationwide program representing over 62,000 college students on over 1100 campuses preparing for careers in education.

Along with NEA's Higher Education program, NEASP is leading the Association's efforts to promote access and affordability in higher education. Rising levels of student debt threaten our members' ability to pursue public service careers in education.

Access and affordability must become a major theme in congressional deliberations on the HEA. We commend the House's step this past January in passing H.R.5, the College Relief Act of 2007, which will cut interest rates in half for subsidized Stafford loans over the next five years. But we must do more and incorporate a comprehensive agenda to increase college access and affordability into the reauthorization of the Higher Education Act. This would include:

- Increase need-based grant aid to restore the purchasing power of the Pell Grant. Immediately Congress should raise the maximum Pell Grant award to $5100.

- Make student loans more affordable by lowering interest rates, by limiting the percentage of income students spend repaying loans and by reinstating the refinancing of existing loans.

- Encourage public service careers by expanding loan forgiveness programs for critical public service careers.

- Cut waste in the student loan programs by passing the Student Aid Reward Act to give money to students and parents, not banks.

We thank you for your consideration on these matters and look forward to future communications on higher education issues.

Sincerely,

Anthony Daniels Jr.,
Chairperson NEA Student Program

LEADERSHIP WITH
RESTRICTED MOBILITY

I had been working tirelessly nonstop to inform student members of the negative impact high college costs and high student loan interest has on the profession of education. I traveled so much that I had to have two fully packed suitcases available at all times, fully stocked with the proper attire. I always kept one in the closet by my front door readily available for the next trip. Sometimes I was overwhelmed and fatigued by the constant traveling, packing, organizing, and conferencing. I rarely ever had downtime or time to relax my mind. Although, I sometimes felt lethargic, I would never rest. I always kept my eye on the prize.

I took a break from traveling and began to prepare for the annual convention for Student Program members, which includes leadership training sessions on topics from assertiveness to management, as well as political action training. Student members were privileged to hear honorable guest speakers, attend an awards banquet, and participate in the *Outreach to Teach* school renovation project. As the Chair of the Student Program, I was responsible for presiding over the entire Student Conference; therefore it was necessary that I prepare.

After a long week of preparation and planning, I participated in the Stoyer wedding as a groomsman in Tennessee. The two individuals getting married were student members within the NEA Student Program who had met the previous year during the NEA Student Leadership Conference in Florida; the year I was elected as Chairman. After leaving the wedding and flying back to D.C., I received a phone call from my fraternity brother Nathan, who lived relatively close to me in Virginia. He was inviting me to play basketball. Nathan and I tried to play basketball on the Sundays I was home. That Sunday, I went home to drop off my things, change clothes, and headed for the basketball court. The basketball court we played on was in an apartment complex on King Street in Alexandria, Virginia.

The teams were 3 on 3 and it was the last game of the day. We were up 14 to 9 and the opposing team had possession of the ball. Throughout the game, I had remained mindful of my weak leg by playing strong mentally. We only needed one more point to win. Josh, who was on the opposing team, attempted to make a three pointer but the ball took a long bounce off the rim back toward the three-point line. There was a high level of suspense. Our team only needed one more basket! We were all playing with a high level of intensity, both mentally and physically. When the ball hit the court, I exerted myself more vigorously, forgetting about my weak leg in great effort to grab the ball. I grabbed the ball and fell to the floor hearing that dreadfully familiar sound of a snap.

I heard snaps and pops and immediately grabbed my ankle. I yelled, "I tore something in my ankle. It hurts really badly!"

While everyone was hovering over me I said, "Please give me some air because I can't breathe with each of you hanging over me." I turned over on my side and felt the coolness of water sink into my basketball shorts, soaking my backside. I had slipped on water. I laid there in agonizing pain with my leg throbbing in a steady pulsation. I was lifted off the court and rushed to the emergency room. I sat in pain as it took several hours for me to be seen by a doctor. I struggled to fight the pain as I filled out forms in order to provide necessary information to the hospital. I had high hopes that my injury would only be minor.

Not long after I gave my information, I was taken back to see a doctor. I was still suffering severe pain. When the doctor arrived, he first asked me about the location of the pain. I told him that the pain was in my ankle. He then applied pressure to my ankle and I shouted, "Doc that hurts really badly! Please be careful!" Instead of honoring my wishes, he again applied pressure to my leg. Again, I shouted, "Doc that hurts really bad. Please be careful!"

Seated in a wheelchair, I was escorted by a nurse to the radiologist for x-rays. Upon arrival I slowly hopped out of the wheelchair, climbed onto the table and stretched out to position myself for the x-ray.

The doctor came back with the results. My fibular was broken in two places and I had a mild sprain in my ankle. I began to think about how this injury would affect the Student Conference. I had to preside over it! With deep concern, I said, "Doc, how long will this take to heal? Will this prevent me from being able to drive or ride on an airplane?"

He replied, "You will have to wear a cast that will be from your hip to the bottom of your foot for about six to nine weeks."

"Doc, not to challenge your opinion, but I have more pain in my ankle than my leg," I said very concerned.

"This is perfectly normal. You twisted your ankle pretty bad but it should be fine in a week," the doctor said assuredly.

After a painful and exhausting day, I finally arrived home. My condo was located on the third floor of the building and there was no elevator. Thankfully, I was able to climb up the three flights of stairs with help from my fraternity brothers. When I finally made it inside, I sat on my couch and began to think about how I was going to survive with a broken leg. Then I thought to myself, "There are people in this world that are in worse conditions; I can't give up!"

On Monday, the next day, I called the NEA's nurse for guidance in seeking a local physician. She provided me with various doctors' names that were covered through my insurance. I made an appointment with one of the local physicians for Wednesday, June 20, 2007. I was stressed. I had a lot on my plate and it was hard to maneuver around my condo. I could only imagine the strife I would face traveling throughout Washington, D.C. I also had obligations to attend to the Student Conference, Saturday June 23, 2007 in Pennsylvania.

After scheduling my doctor's appointment, I hobbled down the stairs to my car and drove to my office. I needed to print off my talking points for the next day at the "Take Back America Conference," which was scheduled for Tuesday. I was assigned to be a panelist in a session that focused on the problems college students face and how we can address them together. The panel was called, "Making College Affordable: The National Imperative." The conference began at 10:00 a.m. in the Washington Hilton. I requested a wheelchair upon my arrival.

When the session began, all of the panelists were to give their opening statements. The panel consisted of the following people: Jen Pae (the United States Student Association President), Tamara Draut (Student Debt Expert), Congressman Joe Courtney and myself. The room was filled with college students and reporters who listened to our dialogue on the issues college students face. After the panel discussion, the panelists had a question and answer session with the audience and the media. When we were finished, I hobbled off the stage back into the wheelchair. As I settled into my wheelchair, several reporters approached me. One asked me, "How many teachers leave the teaching profession within the first five years?" and "What recommendations do you have for Congress?"

"One third of all new teachers leave the teaching profession in the first five years and their reason for leaving is the difficulty to make ends meet. Imagine making $28,000 a year with at least $58,000 in student loan debt. This is not just a burden, it's a barrier. I would like Congress to cut interest on student loans, increase the Pell Grant, and reward those that commit themselves to public service careers such as law enforcement, social work, medicine, education, and firefighting. We should be encouraging public service careers instead of making it difficult for students to go into them. These are some of the critical needs areas that help shape our country. If Congress needs definitive policy suggestions I would be happy to work with them on this."

Following my discussion with reporters, NEA Press Officer, Brian Washington, approached me.

He directed me to attend a radio interview in five minutes with a progressive radio personality. With crutches, I swiftly headed to the radio personalities. They were set up in the lobby area of the Washington Hilton. I hopped from interview to interview. Five different radio hosts interviewed me in regard to the issues of making college affordable and the hardships of No Child Left Behind. I was approached by some bloggers who continued to question the same issues. We continued to discuss these issues in great detail.

It had been a long day. My pain pills began to wear off and the pain started to hit me. Thankfully, all the interviews were finished, so I was able to go back to the NEA building. The trip back to the NEA building was also very trying because we caught a cab. Anyone that rode with me had to sit in the front seat because of the splint I had on my leg. I took my pain medicine as soon as I reached my office.

The following day I attended my scheduled doctor's appointment. The doctor came in and asked, "Where is the pain the worst?"

"My ankle. The doctor in the emergency room said that my leg is broken but my ankle just has a mild sprain," I told him.

The doctor asked his assistant to take x-rays. When the results came back, the doctor told me that I had two torn ligaments in addition to my fibular being broken in two places. This was devastating news for me. I was concerned about my ability to participate in the Student Leadership Conference that Saturday. The doctor informed me that I would need to have the surgery right away before the situation got worst. I asked him if I would be able to fly to Philadelphia on Saturday if I had the surgery that week. I was advised not to fly due to the risk of possibly developing blood clots in my leg at a high altitude. However, he did state that I could ride the train. Therefore, I scheduled the surgery for the next day at 1:00 p.m. The next day, I had surgery and returned to my house later that evening. Since the surgery went well, I was able to go home not long after. Although, I was still a bit drowsy from the anesthesia, I decided to write remarks for the conference. While working on my remarks, one of my fraternity brothers came over to help me pack for the two week conference.

The next day, Nathan came to pick me up and drove me to Union Station in downtown Washington, D.C. An agent with the train station carried my bags through to the terminal area. The nice man waited with me until my train arrived. When it arrived, he helped me to the train in my wheelchair while also assisting me with my bags. He was very kind in offering such wonderful service to me. However, when I got situated on the train, I began to experience challenges. After being on the train an hour, the pain medication started wearing off. I became uncomfortable. Eventually the pain returned fully and I looked around me for an agent on the train. Usually they would walk up and down the aisle to retrieve tickets from the passengers that have recently boarded, but I hadn't seen one for over an hour. Another twenty minutes passed before an agent came up the aisle. I stopped the agent and asked, "Sir, may I please have a glass of water. I need to take my pain pills."

"Yes sir, I will be right back," he answered.

Another hour had passed and still no agent in sight. The pain had severely increased. With only thirty minutes remaining in the trip, the gentlemen had never returned. The train began to slow down and the conductor made the announcement for the next stop, which was my stop. The man finally arrived with the water. I was so irritated and frustrated that he arrived at the last minute but I didn't show it. Instead, I kindly thanked him and then asked him to assist me with my luggage as I departed the train. He helped with one bag but left the other for me to carry, which I found to be a rather difficult task. I waited a long time for someone to come to assist me with my luggage. I was extremely displeased with the lack of intrinsic service I was receiving. For the first time in my life, I was experiencing the world through the eyes of a person with physical disabilities. I was understanding firsthand how important it is to have assistive technology and support for a disabled person trying to live functionally in our society.

I caught a cab to the Radisson Valley Forge Hotel, the host hotel for the Student Leadership Conference. When I reached the hotel, I checked in and rolled myself upstairs to my room. I thought about my agenda and events scheduled for the following morning. I had to prepare for a radio interview in regard to the *Outreach to Teach* project.

In preparation for the conference, I sat in my room revising my talking points for the awards banquet and other general sessions. I was still unable to do much on my own, but I was fortunate enough to have awesome supporters in the Advisory Committee of student members which included, Austin, Dana, Jennie, Don, Sarah O., Sarah T., Todd, Melinda, and Shelia. They were at my side no matter what. In addition to the Advisory Committee members, there were other student members that assisted me as well.

We began the conference with an awards banquet. I experienced more difficulties arriving to the banquet because it was held in a theater, on the bottom floor of the hotel. Unfortunately, at this hotel there weren't any elevators to the bottom floor. Therefore, an employee of the hotel guided me through an alternative route. This alternative route seemed like a maze. We traveled in a downward circular route walking through the hotel kitchens and even through a nightclub to arrive at our destination.

The second day of the conference marked the beginning of the *Outreach to Teach* project, which was held at Gotwals Elementary

School in King of Prussia, Pennsylvania. I started the morning being interviewed by television and newspaper reporters. The reporters were amazed to see that I could be interviewed while standing on one leg after having surgery just days prior. I finished my early interviews and then proceeded to the gym where all the student members, retired teachers, active teachers, and other community volunteers congregated awaiting the exciting project ahead. I entered the gym and began to chant, "Are you ready? Are you ready?" They joyfully shouted, "Yes!"

At Gotwals, the members were assigned particular tasks that included painting, bulletin boards, building walls, laying carpet, and remodeling the teachers' lounge. The groups then proceeded to do their tasks. Throughout the day I went around the school to see if the students needed help with anything, in addition to being interviewed by random reporters. The students were working extremely hard on all the projects. The *Outreach to Teach* project is usually the most rewarding and fulfilling part of the entire Student Conference.

On the last day of the conference, the student members gave me several gifts. One of my favorite gifts to this day is a stuffed giraffe with a bandage on its' leg. I named him Orville. He is a constant reminder of how wonderful people can be when I'm feeling challenged and helpless. I have been blessed to know such amazing people within the Student Program. Receiving Orville, the hurt stuffed giraffe with a bandaged leg, was a touching and humorous gesture. Though my pain and hardships due to the injury were very tough, Orville's presence made it more comforting.

REPRESENTATIVE ASSEMBLY

Immediately after the Student Conference concluded I returned to Washington, D.C. for a post surgery evaluation. Following the evaluation my doctor decided to remove the cast and replace it with a boot. This would give me an opportunity to be more mobile. I would be responsible for wearing this boot until my second surgery. After leaving the doctor's office, I headed back to Pennsylvania to the NEA board meeting before the NEA Representative Assembly.

The Representative Assembly is the NEA's decision-making body. With over 9,000 delegates, it is one of the world's largest democratic, deliberative bodies. During this event, delegates from every state debate issues that impact public education, elect NEA officers, and set policies for the association.

When the Representative Assembly began, I was asked to do the Pledge of Allegiance. This was an awesome responsibility. I got a chance to do the pledge in front of approximately 15,000 people. The crowd included educators from around the country.

In addition to the NEA members, staff and family members of members and staff, there were candidates that were running for President of the United States of America. The first candidate I met was Barack Obama. We met behind the stage in the green room and talked briefly. He asked me the same question as everyone else, "What happened to your leg young man?"

"I injured it playing basketball," I replied.

I then shared my personal story with him of how I got elected to my office, how I've beaten the odds, and how I did what others thought wasn't possible. I told him that he could do the same in the Presidential Election, but advised him to be different from his opponents. He grinned and said, "Thank you for the advice brother." Our conversation had to end do to the large crowds standing and waiting outside the room for pictures.

While others were indifferent about the Senator, I was sold on him from that day forward. In addition to meeting Senator Obama, I also met Governor Mike Huckabee, Senator Christopher Dodd, Senator Joe Biden, and Governor Bill Richardson.

That summer, after the Representative Assembly, I was supposed to travel to Berlin, Germany for the "Education International Conference". The Education International Conference is a teacher union that represents more than 365 countries world-wide, all fighting for global equality for teachers and schools. Unfortunately, following the Representative Assembly, I had a doctor's appointment to determine if it would be safe for me to travel on a plane for more than ten hours. My doctor warned me about possible clots in my ankle. As a result, I contacted the International Relations Department of the NEA to inform them that I was unable to attend the conference. I was slightly disappointed but grateful for all that I experienced.

CLOSING IN ON THE PROMISE

Two weeks later, I was scheduled to speak at the College Democrats of America Conference in Columbia, South Carolina. I took a flight from Washington, D.C. to Charlotte, North Carolina where I met my friend Austin Scott, who accompanied me in the trip from Charlotte to Columbia. After arriving to Columbia, we checked in, took our bags to the room, and headed directly to the conference which took place at the University of South Carolina Student Union. We set up our informational table to distribute literature about the college affordability campaign and the NEA Student Program.

Later that evening, I gave my keynote address to the Black Caucus and other members of the College Democrats of America. Since I was still hurt, I decided that it would be best to do the keynote address sitting down.

The speech was well received. Following the speech, I sat down with the black caucus leadership to discuss ways in which they could expand membership and increase involvement. The following day, Austin and I traveled to Orangeburg, South Carolina, to meet with the Student Government President, Social Committee Chair, Financial Aid, and the Chief of Staff of South Carolina State University. During the meeting, we discussed hosting a college affordability rally at South Carolina State University that fall. The Student Government President volunteered to carry out the responsibilities of hosting the rally. Austin and I left the meeting and headed back to Columbia, feeling good about the opportunity of a rally in the fall.

The next couple of days at the College Democrats of America conference, we continued to collect email addresses at our table. As students were coming by the table, we would inform them about the student loan debt that plagues so many American students and our plan for resolving it. When requesting their active participation in this critical issue, we distributed literature, bracelets, and sold t-shirts. Furthermore, we continued to encourage all the students to participate on the Student Program blog and join the Facebook group. At the conclusion of the conference we evaluated our progress. Austin and I were very pleased with the outcome.

Weeks following the conference, I was due for my second surgery to have the screws removed from my ankle. Shortly after, I went to therapy two to three times a week. I started walking again after the first week of therapy. On September 25, 2007, Don and I traveled down to South

Carolina State University for the College Affordability Rally. The day before this rally, students at South Carolina State University had a pep rally to get fired up. A camera crew also arrived with us to produce a College Affordability video. Don and I helped the students from SCSU take the campaign materials from the boxes and display them on the table. At the rally we had computers set up for cyber-lobbying, tables set up with college affordability shirts, posters, stickers, bracelets and pamphlets. Along with all of the tables containing college affordability materials, we set up a table especially for voter registration.

The student leadership members of South Carolina State University were working diligently to prepare for the day's festivities. I was pleased with the organization and amenities offered at the rally including delicious food and a disc jockey for entertainment after the rally. We were fired up for the rally and to make the day even better, I received great news from Washington, D.C. President Bush signed the College Cost Reduction and Access Act!

It was about 12:30 p.m. when the bill was signed, after the President had previously threatened to veto it. Jeremy Rogers the SGA President led the march and I kept quiet about the bill being signed because I felt that the good news was the perfect ending to the rally.

We began the rally with a march around the campus. We carried signs that stated, "Make College Affordable," while chanting.

"What do we want?" Jeremy would shout.

"Cheap tuition!" we responded.

"When do we want it?" Jeremy followed.

"Now!" we shouted forcefully.

After the march, the program began. The scheduled program included speakers such as: the SGA President, Jeremy Rogers, the South Carolina Education Association Student President, Kareem Benson, and the South Carolina Education Association State Vice President, Kelly Bowers. Each speaker gave their testimony in regard to the issue of College Affordability and how it negatively affects them. After all of the speakers presented their confessions of hardships with student loans and high interest rates, I rose to give my speech.

I started the speech by expressing my appreciation for the opportunity to be present at South Carolina State University. Excitedly, I then shared the great news by announcing, "President Bush signed the College Cost Reduction and Access Act!" They applauded enthusiastically. This was a triumphant feat, which nearly each student member actively and diligently participated in. I continued to praise the student members for their great efforts in this passage of legislation. I asserted that although the bill was signed, we should not become stagnant, but we should continue to fight for the rights of college students across the nation. I emphasized that what we do now, will determine the future for our family and friends. The words of encouragement emanated from within my heart.

Rally Remarks; September 19, 2007

Thank you for this opportunity...

Give yourselves a round of applause for being here today.

I just received word from Washington a couple of minutes ago, that President Bush has signed the College Cost Reduction and Access Act of 2007.Give yourselves a round of applause.

Your presence sends a profound and powerful message to our friends in Washington that you care not just about the issue of college affordability – but also about equality, opportunity and the American dream.

Everywhere I go to talk about this issue – there is a general consensus...the time is right now to turn the page on age old policies...the time is right now to open the doors of opportunity...and the time is right now to do what is right for students all across this nation.

We are fired up
We are fed up and
We need our leaders to fess up to their responsibility to our nation's future.

Because this issue is just as much about college affordability, as it is about accountability.

For over 60 years, our federal government has been shoveling money into programs designed to make college more affordable -- yet a college degree today is more unaffordable than ever.

President after president has declared that, "We must open the door of college to all Americans."

Yet, our elected officials in Washington, with all of their might and wisdom, have <u>poured more fuel onto a fire</u> it was initially determined to put out.

The 109th Congress basically said, "Fend for yourselves American people."

And they backed up their words by:

- Raising interest rates on students loans and
- Cutting $12 billion from the federal student aid program

And because of their obsession with pandering, political posturing and procrastination:

- More than 400,000 college-qualified students were unable to attend a four-year school in 2002 because they couldn't afford it;

- Students are taking out more loans than ever, leading to unmanageable amounts of debt upon graduation;

- Students are delaying major life decisions such as buying a home, starting a family, or pursuing graduate school;

- Federal and state agencies have consistently decreased funding for higher education over the past two decades, as well as shifted from grants to loans; And...

- Over the next decade, 4.4 million high school graduates will not attend four-year colleges and 2 million will attend no college at all.

<u>For these students</u>, the promise of a college education is a hollow one.

<u>For the nation</u>, the loss of human capital will carry us further and further into woes of inequality and lack of opportunity for minority and low-income students.

<u>For the world</u>, they will lose the benefits of our gifts and genius that never had the opportunity to be developed.

<u>The benefits of a college degree is priceless.</u>

Those with bachelor's degrees earn <u>81 percent more</u> than those with high school diplomas.
And over a lifetime, <u>the gap in earning potential exceeds $1 million</u>.

Students from families at the bottom of the economic ladder tend to not finish college and are <u>more likely to be minorities.</u>

Some <u>70 percent of whites</u> go on to college after high school, but only <u>58 percent of black</u> and about <u>53 percent of Hispanic</u> students do.

Despite these challenges, I am hopeful. <u>And you should be too.</u>

In 2006, after the 109th Congress spoke, we spoke even louder at the election polls.

In the 2008 Presidential race, we can't just speak this time.

<u>We must shout!</u>

<u>We must shout</u> so that this time we will not let the enemies of public education <u>snatch victory from our grasp!</u>

<u>We must shout</u> to ensure that our next president is a true <u>friend of public education.</u>

<u>We must shout</u> so that hopes and dreams of all students can be fulfilled.

<u>We must shout</u> so that all election candidates in 2008 join us in making this College Affordability Agenda part of our national commitment to educational excellence.

- Need-based grant aid must be increased to restore the purchasing power of the Pell Grant.
- Student loans must be made more affordable by lowering interest rates, by limiting the percentage of income students spend repaying loans and by reinstating the refinancing of existing loans.
- Public service careers must be encouraged by expanding loan forgiveness programs for critical public service careers.
- Waste in the student loan programs must be cut to give money to students and parents, not banks.

Our goal must be that anyone who's qualified can go to college, regardless of their ability to pay.

Let me tell you another reason why this election is so important.

The next president is likely to appoint 1-3 Supreme Court Justices, whose votes will sway the direction of this country for decades to come.

Race based school assignments, abortion and affirmative action will be impacted by the next appointments.

The Seattle and Louisville cases are just the beginning of a potential wave of decisions that could erode the Brown decision.

We must remain engaged and involved in the process.

And I don't care if you are a Republican or Democrat. <u>This is not about partisan politics.</u>

<u>This is about what is best for public education.</u>

So, if you are not registered, go register today and take a friend.

If you are not engaged, get engaged today.

And if you are not hopeful, find the desire within yourself to make a difference.

Continue to write your letters...making phone calls... petitioning...standing for social justice.

I was pleased to announce the benefits of the College Cost Reduction and Access Act. This bill would provide seven exponential benefits. One benefit includes cutting the interest rate on student loans from 6.8% down to 3.4% over a five-year period of time. The bill also provides new "teach grants" for aspiring teachers correlated with the promise that students will commit to teaching in hard to staff schools in order to qualify for $4,000.00 a year up to four years. Thirdly, the bill expands loan forgiveness programs to students going into public service careers such as: health care, social work, education, law enforcement, and firefighting. The College Cost Reduction and Access Act allow borrowers to repay student loans based on their ability to repay. The bill also provided an increase in the Pell Grant to $5400.00 over the next five years. Providing new tuition assistance grants for qualified undergraduates who commit to teaching in public schools in high-poverty communities or high-need subject area is a sixth benefit of the College Cost Reduction and Access Act. And lastly, the bill creates an Asian American and Pacific Islander Higher Education Serving Institution designation, which will allow eligible schools to improve and expand services for low-income Asian American and Pacific Islander students.

I was proud to be a part of the college affordability campaign which lobbied Congress to increase the Pell grant, provide teach grants, cut interest rates and provide loan forgiveness for public service employees. The College Affordability Campaign consumed me during my term. I became emotionally attached to it. And despite my various challenges including injury, I kept my finger on the pulse. This enabled me to contribute to the hopeful academic future for millions of Americans.

AFTERWARDS

It has been several months since my term ended as the Chairperson of the National Education Association Student Program. During my two-year tenure, I was able to gain knowledge in areas such as the hierarchy of politics, managing conflict through diplomacy, advancing social and political issues, and building strong coalitions.

The title, *To Sweeten Alabama*, is symbolic of the political and social triumphs that my late ancestors endured during the times when Jim Crow laws were in full affect. The title, *To Sweeten Alabama*, is also symbolic of the political and social triumphs that my parents endured during the Civil Rights Movement. As a descendent of my grandparents and parents, I have been blessed to live and grow up in Alabama during the latter part of the twentieth century; at a time when all people regardless of race were encouraged and supported in their pursuit to achieve the American Dream. However, as a child attending public school in Alabama, I too, experienced segregation. Alabama has been steady but slow in its progression both politically and socially. Therefore, with my passion for the state and skills learned while living and working in our nation's capital, I plan to sweeten Alabama.

The actual title of this book derived from a conversation with my close friend, Austin Scott. My initial thought for a title was, "A Story of a Young Man Defying the Odds."

"Why don't you use that as the story line oppose to the actual title?" Austin asked me curiously. He then asked, "Anthony, what do you think about the title, To Sweeten Alabama?"

"Yes, that is an excellent title bro," I replied.

During that moment, the title was born, *To Sweeten Alabama, A Story of a Young Man Defying the Odds.*

I often think about the problems that derive in small communities all around this country. I have become very disheartened, but hopeful about the state of our country's local communities and its negative effects on our youth. Therefore, I decided to commit my life to help promote change. In the words of Gandhi, one must, "Be the change you wish to see in the world."

It was a year ago that I became very interested in learning more about the history of my ancestors. After learning about all their frustration, oppression, heartache, and occasional times of joy, I made a vow to appreciate everyday of my life and embrace each moment. After my revelation, I started to do more for my community and the communities of others. I started to pay close attention to my community and its flaws. The first step to regaining control of a community is to acknowledge that there are problems. We must take the responsibility of what's happening in our communities and stop casting the blame on each other. As I grew up in different communities and households, I found it to be very difficult to be guided in the right direction without a stable example of a positive role model in the community or even close to me. My definition of a positive role model is someone who exemplifies positive, professional, and personal characteristics. John F. Kennedy stated, "The youth of our nation is the clearest mirror of our performance." I truly believe this statement because I have witnessed the negative impact on our youth. Furthermore, I've decided to commit the remainder of my life to being a positive role model to kids all around the nation. Today, children are distracted by so much negativity, in the media, in the community, on the web, in their homes, and sometimes at their schools. As a community, we must realize that a child's mind isn't strong enough to block out all of those negative images that are portrayed.

This is why I believe that I must take the responsibility of being that hope, that inspiration, that motivation, and that positive example to show children that they can in fact, be whatever they want to be regardless of where they're from, what neighborhoods they grew up in, or the choices their parents made. I promise to devote my life to strengthening local communities, starting in Alabama.

REFLECTION OF LEADERSHIP

When reflecting on my term, I believe it to have been very successful for many reasons. I would not have been able to achieve anything without the support of NEA student members, staff, officers, state affiliates, family and friends. The year before I arrived we lost approximately 1,300 members due to the lack of enrollment in education along with competitive organization offerings conflicting with the National Education Association. Consequently, the organization had lost membership because membership had become weak in some areas and non-existent in others. I was elected as the Chairman of the Student Program when student membership was at its' lowest; therefore, people had high expectations and goals set for me, and it was my responsibility to fulfill them. Furthermore, I created goals to increase membership, enhance the quality of teaching, and activate the political activism within the Student Program. Most importantly, I wanted to incorporate lasting programs for the future.

When coming into office, I incorporated a system to improve communication among states by assigning regional caucus chairs, sending out monthly newsletters, speaking to each region, conducting conference calls with state presidents, and having an informal book club discussion. These strategies became very resourceful in order for the Student Program to move beyond status quo. As a result, our membership increased.

The core foundation of any organization is directly related to the state of membership. I made sure that I did everything in my power to provide strategies to increase membership and prevent the numbers from dropping. It has been known that the Student Program Chairperson is judged based upon their ability to increase and retain membership.

Similarly, I too agreed that membership was important, but I also strongly believed as Chairperson that an important aspect of building capacity in an organization was membership retention. Greater contributions could be made in reference to this issue. I could make greater contributions to the organization in addition to this issue. But in order to pursue those other contributions, we needed to tackle the declining student membership. I felt that proactively addressing this issue would be the best approach. In order to move in that direction we needed to offer relevant services for our constituents.

People want to be empowered and know they're apart of something great. I made recommendations for a multi-year dues structure, which focused on freshmen and sophomore recruitment while maximizing exposure externally and internally. A *Rookie of the Year* award was conceived for new members on the state and local level, which would provide new members with initiative and higher interest in leadership. In addition, incorporating a *Rookie of the Year* award would strengthen our local chapters. Providing our organization with maximum exposure was a strategy used to create visibility on campuses across the nation, which inherently led to increased membership.

In addition to focusing on issues at the national level, I also provided strategies to strengthen local chapters. One of the strategies to strengthen local chapters was for them to create an external advisory committee of non-members made up of different majors. My suggestion was for them to recruit Marketing and Advertisement majors to market their meetings, Nursing and Pre-Med students to facilitate a health awareness day and provide health tips to students, and Political Science and Pre-Law students to facilitate and help plan debates for candidates running for local or state office. With the infusion of new and diverse participation within the Student Program, my suggestion to student members was to plan activities in relation to education, including workshops, community outreach, and membership recruitment. These strategies would prove to be very effective on many college campuses nationwide.

Enhancing teacher quality within the Student Program is one of the most important aspects of the Student Program. During my first week in office, I selected a group of student members to identify the weaknesses of first year teachers. This group was also asked to discover improvement strategies in order to assist the first year teachers, which would inevitably improve the quality of teaching for our student members. This group of student members proved to be an essential asset to me during my tenure because I could rely on this group of students for advisement in regard to effective strategies for classroom teachers, which could be incorporated into student conferences and workshops.

I worked very diligently to improve the quality of teaching and competency amongst new teachers within the Student Program. As Chairman of the Student Program, one of my obligations was to serve as a University Accrediting Board Member for the National Council of Accrediting Teacher Education (NCATE). My role was to read the reports of the Board of Examiners along with the reports from various institutions in order to determine whether institutions were properly preparing competent teachers. While serving on this Board, I found a new respect for teacher education programs. I believe that the NCATE process is a necessary and vital process, which helps to enhance the production of highly qualified educators. I believe that every school in the country with a teacher education program should go through a similar process that is nationally accredited. The National Council of Accrediting Teacher Education follows a structured regiment for producing highly qualified and competent teachers to positively benefit every child in America.

Prior to my leadership position in the National Education Association, student members placed a very limited emphasis on politics. Therefore, I asked students around the country to become politically active. I was warned that student members were typically irrelevant, apathetic, and disengaged in regard to political issues, but I refused to accept it. So, as a result, I started asking students to join our text-messaging project, which would provide them with updates about voting and getting friends involved. After the November 2006 elections, we saw an increase in young voter turnout. I strongly believed that college students had become tired of the same old politics and as a result, they became disengaged toward the issues. It was my goal to change this mentality. In response to these apathies, I decided to encourage activism among all student members in regard to the issue of college affordability.

Following the 2006 elections, we transferred the text messaging over to getting our message out about taking action on the College Affordability Campaign. After launching the College Affordability Campaign, students began petition drives, rallies, letter writing campaigns, and donating to the Fund for Children in Public Education. As a result of my influence and their enthusiasm, the Student Program had become one of the strongest voices in the legislative passages of The College Cost Reduction and Access Act. These are examples of the various changes that occurred during my tenure.

Some extraordinary things were accomplished during my tenure, which helped our program grow in numbers and political participation. However, I can say there were difficulties and frustrations, times of indifference, as well as happiness and support. I left my post happier then when I arrived to it. Every day I woke up, I was enthusiastic about going to the office, meetings, or traveling around the country giving speeches, as well as giving and receiving advice. My passion for this organization was great and obvious to many. The hard work and dedication stemmed from my faith, life experiences, stories about my family's perseverance, and the characteristics of determination and competition learned from athletics. My leadership comes from within, but my ability to make others better stems from my years as a point guard. However, without the help from others inside and outside the organization, I would not have been successful. Though this has been an interesting journey, there's still more work to be done throughout this country and the world.

ACKNOWLEDGEMENTS

This book would not have been possible without the love and support of my family and friends.

I want to begin by thanking Jessica Alfonso, one of my friends. She spent months helping me develop this book into what it is. She worked for months diligently and eventually became emotionally attached to this project as if it was her own. During this process, Jessica helped me find my voice by allowing me to articulate myself exactly the way I wanted to express myself through this memoir. I appreciate all of her hard work, dedication, and time committed while she worked tirelessly for long hours as a teacher and as a full time graduate student. She committed many late nights and days to reading and editing this book and for all her assistance I am deeply indebted to her.

Another person of recognition is dedicated to a wonderful man and mentor. I would like to especially thank the Former NEA President Reginald Weaver for writing the foreword to this book. His message set the tone for the rest of the book. I am grateful for his powerful words and wonderful testimony. Reg has been a wonderful and strong influence in my life. I have learned so much from his great character and I have been very privileged to work directly with such an amazing man.

I want to also express my great appreciation to Tanya Wiggins, Aaron Merkin, Jennifer Wentovich, Johnnie Irby, Camillia King, RoSusan Bartee, Thalia Dubose, Daniel Upchurch, Delores Cable, Lashandra Owens, Regina Colston, Felecia Edwards, and Darrell Ezell; all of whom read and provided feedback in regard to the manuscript. These individuals took the time out of their busy schedules to provide me with editorial advice.

I would also like to thank my cousin Tiffany Dubose for editing, reading, and interviewing my Uncle Willie Dubose and two of my aunts, Barbara Simpson and Lizzie Dubose. I would be remised if I didn't thank my family members for giving Tiffany the information needed, which helped me develop the introduction.

Last but not least, I would like to thank Therman Evans for his mentoring, coaching, and guidance in this project. It was because of him that I revealed every detail regardless of public perception. He too became emotionally attached to this project. Sometimes I believed that Therman was more excited about this book than I was. I am also greatly indebted to his services and support, and will be forever grateful.

Special thanks to the following organizations for their continued advocacy and support

Calvary Baptist Church
Merritt Elementary School
Shelly Boone Middle School
Bullock County High School
Alabama Agricultural & Mechanical University
Alabama Education Association (AEA)
Student Alabama Education Association (SAEA)
National Education Association (NEA)
National Education Association Student Program (NEA-SP)
National Council for the Accreditation of
Teacher Education (NCATE)
Kappa Alpha Psi Fraternity, Inc.
United States Student Association (USSA)
The Roosevelt Institute
United States Hispanic Leadership Institution (USHLI)
American Medical Student Association (AMSA)
Campus Progress
Black Youth Vote (BYV)
Campaign for America's Future
Young People for the American Way
1Sky
Young Voter Pac

Stay Connected by:

Joining our facebook page:
http://www.facebook.com/pages/Anthony-Daniels/76403102411
Following me on twitter:http://twitter.com/AnthonyDaniels

Manufactured By: RR Donnelley
Momence, IL USA
February, 2011